CONSERVATIVE CONFIDENTIAL

Scott:
Please enjoy!

FRED

Fred Litwin

Fred Litwin is a marketing and sales professional who worked nine years for Intel Corporation in England, Singapore and Hong Kong. In 1998-1999, Fred managed a team of twenty people organizing the launch of the Pentium III microprocessor in Asia.

In 2000, he founded NorthernBlues Music, a cutting-edge label dedicated to stretching the boundaries of the blues. To date, the company has released over 70 CDs, and has garnered twelve Juno Award nominations in Canada and over forty Blues Music Award nominations in the United States.

In 2007, Fred started the Free Thinking Film Society in Ottawa to showcase films on liberty, freedom and democracy. The Society has now shown over 100 films and also organizes book launches and panel discussions.

Conservative Confidential: Inside the Fabulous Blue Tent is his first book and you can find updates and pictures at ConservativeConfidential.com.

CONSERVATIVE CONFIDENTIAL

INSIDE THE FABULOUS BLUE TENT

FRED LITWIN

First edition published in 2015 by NorthernBlues Books

Cover design by Kathleen Lynch
Edited by Benita Mehta

FIRST EDITION

Litwin, Fred
Conservative Confidential
ISBN - 978-0-9948630-0-3

Dedicated to the memory of Christopher Hitchens

After 9/11, when many of my friends were questioning the fight against the Taliban in Afghanistan; when so many people were wondering if Osama bin Laden was really behind 9/11; when it seemed that the mere mention of the name George Bush prompted an immediate allergic reaction; and when that ridiculous slop called *Fahrenheit 9/11* seemed to be in every cinema, it was calming to know that Christopher Hitchens had my back.

Contents

Introduction

"Is Canada Run By A Gay Mafia?"

That was the headline on a Vice.com article from July 5, 2013. I, Fred Litwin, know the answer to that question. The answer is. . . . no, not really. But the true story is a lot more interesting, and that story is what this book is about.

What's been going on in Canada's conservative movement, and inside the Conservative Party, will surprise a lot of Canadians. What's been going on inside the Left will come as a shock to a lot of people, too. And what's been going on inside the gay leadership will probably even astound gay people. What the big city media has been up to — particularly the corporate management of the CBC — is downright disturbing.

This book is about all those things, and more. There are intrigues with the Iranian embassy. There's the serial fabricator Michael Moore. There's the vulgar American loudmouth Ann Coulter, there's the decrepit counterculture guru Noam Chomsky, and there's a particularly obnoxious right-winger named Pamela Geller you'll meet in an entire chapter on the nasty "counter-jihad" subculture within the conservative movement.

There are also the twists and turns of my own personal journey. The story opens on Sept. 11, 2001, and I bet the way it unfolds, and the way it ends, will cause a lot of people to say: hey, that's my story, too.

But some people will not be happy with this book at all, so it's probably best to start with some "trigger warnings."

If you're a Conservative you might find the last few chapters upsetting. I don't know if they will make you angry but if you are looking for a "safe space," just read the first half of the book. It's because of the first half that a lot of "progressives" will be even angrier with me, so my advice to them: If you're the daring sort and you think you can handle the odd "micro-aggression" here and there, then read all the way through. If you stick it out, you might actually end up liking the last chapters.

Consider this book as a kind of "coming out" story. Coming out is something I've had to do my entire life. When I finally came out as a gay man in the early 1980s, it was a daunting task, but it turned out to be far easier than I expected. Coming out years later as a conservative proved far more vexing.

It would be hard for most people to imagine how lonely it was to be gay when I was a boy. As my hormones raged in high school in the 1970s, I found myself completely isolated. I always knew I was different. My friends couldn't stop talking about girls, and since I really had absolutely no interest, I was just silent. I'd always try to change the topic — movies, television, or hockey — but that only takes you so far. The conversation would inevitably come back to girls. I would just go back into my shell and feel incredibly awkward.

There were no gay characters on television or in the movies. There was really no "gay" anything. Every time I saw a cute boy, I couldn't say a word. I even had to be careful about noticeably turning my head. As recently as the 1960s, when I was in my early teens, homosexual acts were offences under the Criminal Code, and gay people were further liable to be considered "criminal sexual psychopaths" and subjected to indefinite prison terms. In 1959, the RCMP set out on a national investigation to identify homosexuals in Canada, with a particular focus on the federal civil service. A 1960-61 report found 560 federal employees who were believed to be gay. The next year, another 300 federal employees were added to the list, along with 2,000 homosexuals who were employed outside the federal civil service. By the following year, the RCMP had enlisted the support of local police force "morality squads." In 1964-65, there were 6,000 homosexuals in RCMP files. The number rose to 7,500 in the next year. By 1967-68, the RCMP had accumulated 9,000 files on suspected homosexuals, one-third of whom were federal employees.

To aid in its mission, the RCMP developed the "Fruit Machine," which tested pupil dilation when showing individuals pictures of naked men and women. If the pupil dilated when showing pictures of the same sex, then that person would be deemed homosexual. As word got out that the RCMP was testing people, it became very hard to get people to take the test. Even if you were straight, a false positive could destroy your career. A report on file with the Canadian Museum of History estimates that at least 100 employees lost their jobs as a result of the machine's testing.

Homosexuality wasn't decriminalized in Canada until the Trudeau government changed the laws in 1969, but long after that, Canadian society was still hostile to gay people. In the 1970s, many newspapers, including the Toronto Star, had a ban on gay advertisements, and gay people were prohibited from even entering Canada. Gays could not serve in the military until 1992. Gay bookstores were continually harassed and fought continual battles with Canada Customs. Gays were bashed, and gay teenagers routinely committed suicide. Throughout the 1970s and into the early 1980s, gay bars and baths throughout the country were raided by police and hundreds of gay people were arrested. The American Psychiatric Association removed homosexuality as a mental disorder in 1973, but the Canadian Psychiatric Association followed suit only in 1982, and the Province of Alberta only in 2010. Doctors in Alberta reportedly billed for "treating" homosexuality in more than 1,700 cases between 1995 and 2004.

Coming out as a Conservative in the first decade of the 21st century, a lot of my friends treated me like I was crazy. I faced a wall of disbelief. "How on earth could you be a Conservative? You're gay," people would tell me — as if all gay people think the same way. I was told I suffered from "false consciousness." I never lost a friend by coming out as a gay person, but I lost friends coming out as a Conservative. As recently as July 2014, a longtime friend in the music industry said it was time for us to "totally part company." He was upset that I had been critical of Barack Obama. "The basic disconnect between [Prime Minister Stephen] Harper's moralistic smugness and that fact that you're gay is a mystery I simply can't fathom."

Maybe this book will help unravel the mystery. Maybe there are a lot of things that this book might help shed some light on. That's my hope, anyway.

One

The World Turned Upside Down

Sept. 11, 2001

The phone rang at about 8:45 in the morning. It was my friend Janet Fiabane. She told me that a plane had just hit the World Trade Center.

I was at home in Ottawa and I'd just finished breakfast. I was headed upstairs to my home office when she called. At first, I thought maybe a Cessna had accidentally hit one of the towers. I'd known that in the 1940s a plane had hit the Empire State Building and several people had died. Maybe this was the same kind of thing.

It took about 15 or 20 minutes of checking in with the news on the internet before it became obvious that something really big was happening. I can't recall exactly what it was — the second plane hitting the other tower? — but I hurried downstairs to the living room to watch it all unfold on television. I was transfixed. I couldn't get up from the couch. At about 10 o'clock, the South Tower fell. I sat there in disbelief. People were being murdered right before my eyes.

The North Tower fell about a half hour later. The smoke billowed. People were running away. What would happen next? Nobody knew.

No matter which channel I turned to — CNN, CTV, CBC, ABC, CBS, NBC — nobody had any idea what had really happened. No one seemed able to get a grasp on the totality of what was going on. What expert or talking head could they turn to?

I was silent most of day. I called my office in Toronto — my record company, NorthernBlues Music. I exchanged a few words with my office manager Pamela Brennan about how horrible it all was. I called a few friends. Have you seen the news? What could one say? Every now and then I'd managed to get up from the couch, dash upstairs and check my office email and then run back downstairs again so I wouldn't miss anything important.

I'd lived in New York for more than six years, between 1985 and 1991, and I worked on Wall Street. I was worried about two close friends. Barry Godin lived on Christopher Street in the heart of Greenwich Village and worked at a bizarre movie-prop warehouse in midtown Manhattan. Judd Silverman was an aspiring playwright who lived in Brooklyn, but he worked in the financial industry, sometimes in the Wall Street district, and it wouldn't be unusual for Judd to be in the World Trade Center or at least in the vicinity.

I'd heard on CNN that the telephone circuits were clogged so I probably couldn't get through if I tried and they probably wouldn't be home anyway, so I sent them emails. I was relieved when I heard back from them both quickly. They were okay. Barry ended up doing a lot of volunteer work at Ground Zero helping the police and fire crews.

When another passenger plane was flown into the Pentagon, and then another plane crashed in a field in Shanksville, Pennsylvania, I was paralysed. I ended up on the couch all day. There was no way of knowing if or when something big might happen again and I couldn't take my eyes off the television. I could barely bring myself to make lunch. The hours ticked by. It was everything I could do to make myself some dinner. It made me wonder if I should have a television in the kitchen.

What justification could anyone ever use for such a monstrous attack? How could anybody take credit for what had happened? Who could even think of such a crime?

Right from the start, there was speculation linking the atrocities that day back to Osama bin Laden and his Al-Qaida network. I'd never heard of Al-Qaida, or if I had, I'd forgotten. I was dimly aware of bin Laden, probably from the time then-President Bill Clinton bombed what turned out to be an innocent pharmaceutical factory in Khartoum,

Sudan, in retaliation for bin Laden's direction of bomb attacks on the U.S. embassies in Kenya and Tanzania. I was also aware of the Al-Qaida attack on the destroyer USS Cole in 2000 as it lay at anchor in Aden Harbour in Yemen. But I had no idea the terrorist threat was anywhere near as grave as it turned out to be.

There were so many questions and so few answers, but one thing I figured was certain was that this was a time to stand with the United States. Over the next few days it was encouraging to see people all over the world come together and reach out to Americans in their time of grief.

In New York, the courage of the police and the firefighters really stood out. Christie Blatchford had travelled to New York to cover the story for the National Post. I clipped her story and I still had it years later. "They were unyielding, and yet not stupidly stoic; I cannot count the number of times I saw firemen or police officers wrap their arms around one another or clamp big hands to one another's shoulders, and often saw tears behind goggles once or twice streaming down grime-covered cheeks. They were affectionate and tender with each other, but strong and fierce in their resolve."

New Yorkers came together. The world watched, and it was great to see Canada step up. More than 75,000 Canadians signed up to give blood. Two hundred and twenty-four passenger planes were diverted to Canadian cities like Halifax and Gander and 30,000 stranded Americans found temporary homes here in Canada. In those first few hours and days, Prime Minister Chretien said all the right things. He made sure that Americans knew that Canada was with them all the way.

On the evening of Sept. 11, President George Bush — I hadn't exactly been a fan of his and I'd rooted for Al Gore in 2000 — seemed to have found his voice. His short speech was strong and quite moving. "None of us will ever forget this day. Yet, we go forward to defend freedom and all that is good and just in our world." New York Mayor Rudy Giuliani was similarly inspiring. He didn't just sit around in an office. He was right there at the centre of the action. The tone he took in answering the press was right and proper. He gave every impression of being totally in control. By rallying New Yorkers, he rallied the country. Bush's bullhorn speech to emergency rescue workers at the site was just two minutes long but it packed a wallop. He got it just right. He knew how to talk to the firefighters, the police officers and everyone else trying to pick up the pieces.

Prime Minister Chretien proclaimed Friday, Sept. 14 a national day of mourning in Canada. More than 100,000 people crowded Parliament Hill. Police had planned for only about 15,000 or 20,000, but people just kept on coming. The main doors of the American Embassy on Sussex Drive were piled high with flowers, trinkets and messages.

But then something strange happened. A little more than a week after those crowds on Parliament Hill, President Bush addressed a joint session of Congress, singling out several countries for their support. He thanked Britain, South Korea, Australia, Egypt and France, but unfortunately he left out Canada. It was a minor slip-up — the president's speechwriters had forgotten to mention Canada, and by the time they remembered it was too late to change the speech. But to a lot of Canadians, it was a snub. An insult. An unconscionable affront. The news media busied itself with hand-wringy accounts of Canadian sensibilities having been once again offended by something an American president had said or done, in this case having not said and not done. It was embarrassing. Something strange was going on.

I'd been away from Canada for nearly 17 years. I left in 1983, spent a year travelling the world, worked in New York City for more than six years, then in England for three and a half years, then nearly six years in Singapore and Hong Kong. When I finally settled down in Ottawa in 2000, it was weird, reading stories in a Canadian newspaper I'd never read before (the National Post) about a Canadian political party I'd never heard of before (the Canadian Alliance). But I'd grown up in Montreal, went to university there and in Kingston, and I'd started out my career on Bay Street in Toronto, so it didn't take long to re-adjust. Not long after I moved to Ottawa I took up my passion for music. After backing the folk label Borealis Records, in March 2001 I started up my own NorthernBlues label. Things were moving along nicely. I had no idea that my life would soon take a different kind of course altogether. I didn't know it then, but that morning in September was the turning point.

Like everyone else I knew, I was shaken to the core that morning. How could anybody fly planes into buildings like that? What kind of monsters were these people? What kind of ideology would counsel the deliberate murder of thousands of innocent civilians? Whoever the perpetrators were, what kind of hatred had taken hold of these people?

My instincts told me to turn to the Left for answers. Although I'd built a career from investment analyst and venture capital consultant to a position as a division manager for Intel, the world's leading manufacturer of computer chips, I'd always been a man of the Left. I was a precocious kid from a liberal Jewish household in Montreal's Notre-Dame-de-Grâce — when I was 12, I held a firm view favouring Paul Martin Sr. in the 1968 Liberal Party leadership race because he was strong on foreign policy. But I got swept up in Trudeaumania like everyone else. That was the year before my father died.

After high school, I passed on Vanier College because I figured it would be overrun by cliquey Jews from upscale Hampstead, and chose Dawson College instead. It was a long bus ride and five subway stops away, but everything was taught from a socialist perspective. I loved it. The Sociology of Leisure and Sport taught us about the racism in professional sports. Propaganda and Advertising taught us about how corporations tell lies. In Children's Literature, we learned how to recognize the ways that children's stories serve the ruling class. I remember learning about how multinationals had ruined making meals for families by having all these newfangled processed foods. World Politics finally gave me an anti-American view of what was going on. It was all of a piece with the times. It was great.

Despite my socialist leanings, I decided to study business, mostly because my brother-in-law Ron Levy had earned an MBA from Wharton in Philadelphia, and so I wanted one too. I always thought that at least socialists would want well-run factories. The Sir George Williams campus of Concordia University in Montreal had a really good business school, so that's where I went. The Commerce department was housed in a building next to the YMCA on Drummond Street. But it was a good school. From there I went to Queens University in Kingston, where I got my MBA. Along the way, I'd organized protests, led an occupation of a college library, and failed miserably as a student politician. After I got my degree I was an anti-nuclear activist, attended every demonstration I could, came out as a gay man and threw myself into the life of a committed left-wing activist. This wasn't always easy, working for The Man. But I managed.

So in the days after 9/11, I expected the Left would rise to the occasion and come up with some worthwhile explanations, some reasonable analysis, some idea of what it all meant, some leadership on the right thing to do. But straight off the mark, the Left offered a quick, easy, knee-jerk response. No thought went into any of it. It was all America's fault.

I certainly couldn't claim any useful knowledge of the history of Afghanistan. I knew the Taliban were medieval sadists. I knew a little bit about the CIA-led war against the Russians in Afghanistan in the 1980s, but I knew nothing about Afghanistan's Northern Alliance anti-Taliban resistance and its gallant leader, Ahmad Shah Massoud. I knew next to nothing about the Pakistani Intelligence Services and its meddling in Afghan affairs, and about as much about Al-Qaida's role in it all. So for me, 9/11 was time to show a bit of humility, to take some time to think, to read, and to learn more about what had really happened. My enquiries ended up coinciding with an exercise in soul-searching that had begun to occupy a lot of my time. I didn't fully realize it then, but by 9/11 I was already well on the way to becoming a desperately disillusioned "progressive." I'd become entranced by a book, *The Politics of Bad Faith* by David Horowitz. It had shaken me up. Here was a really smart guy — a lifelong, prominent and influential lefty — and by the 1990s he was embroiled in a total rethinking and revisiting of left-wing politics.

Horowitz's parents had been Communists — he was a "red diaper baby," as such kids were called at the time. In 1968, Horowitz was named co-editor of Ramparts, arguably the most influential left-wing American magazine of the time. And he'd become a conservative. *The Politics of Bad Faith* was a small paperback collection of essays. I couldn't put it down. Horowitz was scathing in his criticisms of what had become of the Left after the fall of communism. Postmodern leftism had been reduced to a "theoretical expression of agnostic nihilism." So-called critical theory, deconstructionist analysis and cultural determinism — with its inordinate emphasis on ethnicity and race — all led to assaults on freedom and liberty. The whole thing amounted to a "rejection of the concept of the individual." Left-wing ideas had become rife with "direct echoes of the fascist theories of the 1930s." The cultural revolution of the 1960s — the subject of Horowitz's earlier book, *Destructive Generation* — had led to a complete transformation of university curricula. Great books were out. Minor works were in, as long as they were about colonialism, racism or the evils of capitalism. The crimes of socialist countries like Vietnam, Cuba, Nicaragua and North Korea were to be ignored.

Horowitz argued that it all added up to a "radical assault on America's future." This was perhaps a bit over the top, but it made for stirring stuff. I was bewitched. *The Politics of Bad Faith* challenged everything about my outlook. It also confirmed what I had only just begun to suspect about my own politics. By 9/11, I had been back in Canada for little more than a year, and it was as though I was watching Horowitz's nightmare future play out right before my eyes.

Everybody seemed to be obsessed with identity politics. A term I had never heard before — "visible minority" — had become a kind of mantra. It's not that I was against going to great lengths to help, say, aboriginal people or disabled workers. And it wasn't just because I was a white male, but the obsession with skin colour and gender seemed to substitute the principle that merit should be the foremost consideration in employment with extremely complex affirmative action rules.

The Employment Equity Act of 1995 designated women, people with disabilities, aboriginal people and visible minorities as being entitled to preferential hiring within the civil service and federally regulated industries. I'd found myself wondering why I didn't qualify. If I wore the right clothes and put on a yarmulke, wouldn't I be a visible minority, too? When I had a beard back in the 1980s, people used to say that I looked like a rabbi, particularly when I wore a corduroy jacket. I was gay, too. Why wasn't I on some hire-first list?

It was because visible minorities were defined in law as "persons who are non-Caucasian in race or non-white in colour." This meant that two immigrants from Latin America, arriving in Canada at exactly the same time, would be treated completely differently depending on their skin colour. Historically, Jews had been a persecuted minority, but our skin colour meant that there would be no hiring preference for us. And what about the children of mixed marriages? I came to conclude that sooner or later, more rules and regulations would be needed to determine if people had the proper credentials to qualify as a visible minority, and the only people left out would be white males.

The absurdity of identity politics first hit home with one of the first artists I'd signed to my record label, NorthernBlues Music. Otis Taylor, an African-American from Colorado, came to me with a fully-produced CD that he wanted to release, titled *White African*. Otis's blues were stark and hypnotic, no drums but a droning bass line that reverberated throughout the album. His lyrics were all about the black experience of slavery, oppression, Jim Crow, segregation and racism. It was a great record.

When *White African* was ready for release, I called Otis and asked him if we should send it out to black radio stations across the United States. He laughed and said, no, the music was meant for a white audience, specifically National Public Radio listeners. Guilty white people. Not surprisingly, NPR and its listeners absolutely ate up the CD. It was nominated for Album of the Year at the 2002 W.C. Handy Blues

Music Awards in Memphis.

Meanwhile, the feminist movement was moving away from the great cause of equality of opportunity and into something that often seemed more like anti-male frenzy, or at least a critique of the essential nature of men. At the annual "Take Back the Night" marches, the speeches and rhetoric clearly focused on the threat women faced from men while walking alone at night. But the marches had originated in the inner cities of the United States in the 1970s — a radically different kind of environment than the exceedingly safer streets of Canadian cities by the first decade of the 21st century. Some of the Canadian marches barred men on the grounds that their involvement would intrude upon the safe space women were entitled to, further entrenching the idea that men, generally, pose a threat to women.

It was also occurring to me that there was something odd about the gay community's approach to AIDS. During its ghastly zenith, AIDS cases in Canada peaked in 1993 with 1,826 cases. But safe sex, sex education and maybe even something in the virus itself had brought AIDS cases down to 481 in 2000 and 385 by 2001 (within a decade, the number of AIDS cases had halved again). Deaths were also dramatically declining, from 1,500 in 1995 to 258 in 2000.

I'd started to wonder if AIDS was really still the greatest health threat to gay people, and whether the gay community leadership was justified in its loud and constant demands for government attention to the issue. I'd started going back to gay bars, and everybody seemed to be smoking. You could barely breathe. All you had to do was to look at the annual death statistics, do some quick calculations and you'd see that smoking was causing far more deaths within the gay community than AIDS.

By 2000, the AIDS crisis was at its most acute in Africa, and African women were at great risk. Canadian AIDS activists could have mounted campaigns to win federal support for African communities fighting the virus. But, the Canadian gay community seemed completely uninterested.

At an AIDS rally I attended in the summer of 2001 there was a booth set up specifically to promote the message that Canadian women, too, were at risk of contracting AIDS. During the days of the Reagan administration, there was some tactical sense in promoting the idea that everyone — not just gay people — was at some risk of contracting AIDS. But in Canada in the year 2000, only 33 women were among the AIDS deaths recorded that year. At the height of the epidemic in 1995, 1,383 Canadian men died, while only 104 women died.

And then there was the gorilla in the room: Israel. Throughout most of its young life, Israel had been the darling of the Left. The country was founded by socialist atheists who believed that a Jewish homeland was the only reasonable answer to the vicious anti-Semitism that haunted Jews across Europe. For decades, the country's politics had been dominated by the labour movement, its political party and its socialist kibbutzim. The Israeli Labour Party and its allies were proud and active members of the Socialist International. By the morning of Sept. 11, 2001, Israel was the Left's global arch-villain, often even beating out the Great Satan, America.

Things started to unravel in the mid-1950s, when the Soviet Union, after initially backing Israel and voting for the partition of Palestine in 1947, realigned itself with Egypt and the Arab world. Vicious anti-Zionism campaigns became part of the Soviets' Cold War strategy. After 1967, when Israel won a war against several neighbouring Arab states, the duty to demonize Israel gradually became an article of faith for the 1960s' New Left. The Palestinians, under the cunning leadership of Yasser Arafat, got the message and re-branded themselves as part of the oppressed Third World.

The 1993 Oslo peace process made things seem like peace was within reach. The summit at Camp David in 2000 was a dramatic surge for peace — Ehud Barak, the Israeli Prime Minister, made huge concessions, and the Americans tried hard to bridge the gaps between the two sides. But Arafat turned down all the proposals and never once made a counter-offer. The summit ended in disaster. Soon after, under the pretext of Ariel Sharon's visit to the Temple Mount, the bloody "second intifada" began, with all its terror bombings of buses, restaurants and weddings. Life in Israel was hell.

Campuses across North America started to explode in protests — not in response to Palestinian terrorism, but against the "apartheid state," Israel. The anti-Zionist narrative of what by then was a "postmodern" Left had taken hold. Israel could do no right.

Just three days before 9/11, the United Nations' World Conference against Racism in Durban, South Africa degenerated into a festival of anti-Zionist (and even anti-Semitic) hysterics. The 19th century anti-Semitic fabrication, The Protocols of the Learned Elders of Zion, was circulated. Protestors carried placards comparing Israel to the Nazis. The conference NGO Forum issued a declaration that Israel was a "racist, apartheid state" and accused Israel of "racist crimes including war crimes, acts of genocide and ethnic cleansing." The American and the Israeli delegations walked out. The Canadian delegation, led by Hedy Fry, the federal Secretary of State for Multiculturalism and the Status of Women, chose to stay.

Only two days after 9/11, the Toronto Star's Haroon Siddiqui was already wondering whether the attacks occurred because America was "indifferent to the suffering of too many peoples, from Afghanistan to Chechnya to the Middle East. . . thus driving the ordinary folk there to seethe in silence against America and the crazed ones into fanatical acts."

On Sept. 19, Siddiqui had decided that the 9/11 attacks were due to "American complicity in injustice, lethal and measurable, on several fronts," including the Israeli-Palestinian conflict, the economic sanctions on Iraq, American alliances with the governments of Algeria, Turkey and Egypt, and "the mess in Afghanistan where the CIA recruited and trained the likes of bin Laden" (which was untrue; Osama bin Laden was never a trainee, client or asset of the CIA, of any description). Siddiqui concluded that the public, more than the media, "senses" this. "Some put it crudely: America had it coming."

Around the same time, the noted left-wing journalist Robert Fisk
wrote: "This is not the war of democracy versus terror that the world will
be asked to believe in the coming days. It is also about American missiles
smashing into Palestinian homes and U.S. helicopters firing missiles
into a Lebanese ambulance in 1996 and American shells crashing into
a village called Qana and about a Lebanese militia paid and uniformed
by America's Israeli ally hacking and raping and murdering their way
through refugee camps."

The Toronto Globe and Mail's Rick Salutin wrote that 9/11
was a consequence of the United States having nurtured Islamic
fundamentalism in Afghanistan, "in the course of which it worked with,
armed and trained — Osama bin Laden!" Except, again, this is untrue.
Salutin's solution: end the Israeli occupation of Palestinian lands and
end the sanctions against Saddam Hussein's Iraq.

In the Ottawa Citizen, the day after the atrocities in New York and
Washington and the sky above Shanksville, Pennsylvania, Susan Riley
wrote that it was worth asking whether the attacks "had anything to do
with the recent UN conference on racism and the United States' refusal
to join the chorus against Israel." But she noted that Canadians didn't
have anything to worry about. "We are safe, because of our relative
harmlessness, more than our virtue."

In the Globe and Mail on Sept. 14, Naomi Klein, asked whether
U.S. foreign policy created "the conditions in which such twisted logic
could flourish, a war not so much on U.S. imperialism but on perceived
U.S. imperviousness?" A few days later, she wrote that Osama bin Laden
was a "figure of diabolical fanaticism," who was at the same time "the
warped and twisted progeny of all of these unintended consequences of
wars past and present — a Frankenstein of collateral damage."

I'd gone looking for an explanation from the Left, and there it was.
America had it coming.

One of my more thoughtful friends at the time was Gerry Toomey,
a consultant for international aid organizations. We exchanged several
emails debating what should be done. Gerry was concerned that a global

coalition against terrorism might not distinguish "between revenge and deterrence, guilt and innocence, and hypocrisy and justice." He was worried about the people in Afghanistan who were dependent on foreign aid, which could be disrupted to tragic consequence by war. Gerry was struggling with the question of what to do, and his concerns were reasonable. But he was an anomaly.

To the extent that the Left had any answers, they were simple. Confront Israel. Free Saddam Hussein's Iraq from sanctions. Get out of the Middle East. These were also among Al-Qaida's dozens of demands, which included quite a few that were also much the same as the boilerplate demands of the Left. No wonder then that the Left would have a hard time articulating a challenge to Al-Qaida's program. But was giving in to Osama bin Laden the answer?

On Oct. 1, Sunera Thobani, a university professor and former president of the National Action Committee on the Status of Women, delivered a fiery speech to 500 delegates at an Ottawa conference titled Women's Resistance: From Victimization to Criminalization. Thobani answered the what-to-do question through the lens of identity politics. She titled her talk "If We Are All Americans Now, What is a Brown Girl to Do?" Thobani said that the "path of U.S. foreign policy is soaked in blood," so the United States should submit to three "demands": lift the sanctions on Iraq, resolve the Palestinian question, and remove American military bases in the Middle East.

In attendance at the Ottawa conference was Status of Women minister Hedy Fry, who'd stuck around at Durban while the U.S. and Israel were walking out. Fry was on the podium while Thobani was talking. She did not walk out. To his credit, Prime Minister Chretien said it was "a terrible speech that we are 100 percent against."

Then, as an exemplar of the crazier reaches of the far Left, University of Ottawa professor Michel Chossudovsky, offered an analysis that was tellingly consistent with liberal-left mainstream views. His first essay after 9/11, published on his own conspiracy-theory aggregation effort (the Centre for Research on Globalisation), was titled "Osamagate." It was a connect-a-dot exercise purporting to show linkages between bin Laden and the CIA.

Meanwhile, in the real world, President Bush was biding his time. He demanded that the Taliban hand over Osama bin Laden and expel Al-Qaida. The Taliban refused. On Oct. 7, 2001, the United States and Britain began Operation Enduring Freedom by bombing Taliban positions. On Nov. 12, Northern Alliance forces marched into Kabul, and the Taliban fled. By December, the UN Security Council had established the International Security Assistance Force (ISAF) to oversee Kabul operations. Eventually, more than 50 countries, including Canada, would join in military operations in Afghanistan.

Throughout this, President Bush seemed measured. He certainly wasn't reckless. Nobody was being bombed back into the Stone Age.

Sometime in late November, I walked into Book City on the Danforth, one of my favourite bookstores in Toronto, and out on the front counter was a special display with Noam Chomsky's "9-11." It was a 125-page pamphlet containing several interviews Chomsky had given related to the atrocities of Sept. 11. The management of Book City clearly thought this was a book everybody would want to read. It was a bestseller in five countries and set sales records for its publisher, Seven Stories Press. I'd once been a huge Chomsky fan.

I picked up a copy and looked through it. It was all typical Chomsky — bash Israel, bash American foreign policy, blame the United States for Al-Qaida, condemn the United States as a terrorist state — all 21st century regurgitations from the 1960s. I sighed and put the book back.

I was done with the Left.

Two

Into the Wilderness

The weeks and months following Sept. 11, were a very tough period for me. Ever since 9/11, I'd been disoriented. I'd started losing friends; I'd find myself having horrendous email fights about politics. Fortunately, I was working extremely hard managing NorthernBlues. I was on the road for much of the year, and it kept my mind occupied.

The "intifada" had started just before 9/11 and it had become increasingly bloody. This was actually the "second intifada;" the first being mainly a stone-throwing affair in the late 1980s that ended with the Oslo Accords of 1993. This time around, cafes, restaurants and buses were being blown up all over Israel. It was good to have something that kept my mind off things. I used to travel from Ottawa to the NorthernBlues office in Toronto almost every week, and I'd been named to the Board of Directors of the Blues Foundation in Memphis, an organization dedicated to promoting blues music as an art form.

I had to be at board meetings, attend the annual blues music awards and travel to various blues festivals throughout North America. Meanwhile, the situation in Israel was leaving me inconsolable. The Israelis were digging in. They'd started on the construction of "the wall" to seal off Israel from the West Bank, and when the IDF was sent in April 2002 into Jenin to clear out a large concentration of Arab jihadist and PLO fighters, a rumour spread around the world that hundreds of civilians had been massacred. Throughout Europe and North America, protests erupted. It was as though everybody was against Israel.

I remember hiking in the Gatineau Hills in Quebec with my friend

Janet Fiabane — it was Janet who'd called me on the morning of 9/11 and told me to turn on my TV — and when I mentioned how horrified I was at the suicide bombings in Israel, she replied, well, what else can they do? I just dropped the subject. Friends I had known for years were happy to criticize Israeli Prime Minister Ariel Sharon but were strangely silent about Arafat's ultra-violent and obscene second intifada. At one point, at my boyfriend Andrew's parents' house, I found myself almost in tears trying to get them to understand why Israel deserved defending, and why events in Israel had left me so upset.

In September 2002, at Concordia University in Montreal, a riot broke out, preventing Benjamin Netanyahu from giving a speech to students (Netanyahu was Israel's foreign minister at the time). About 650 students, most of them Jews, were stuck inside the auditorium and had to be escorted out by the police in groups of ten. In Canada, Israel was now the subject of sullen antipathy, at best. At its worst, it was anti-Semitic venom packaged as anti-Zionism. Canada would go on to be the birthplace of Israel Apartheid Week, an annual event that began at the University of Toronto in January 2005 and eventually involved anti-Israel teach-ins and protests in 55 cities around the word.

Everywhere I turned, people were worked up about Israel. And nobody, particularly on the Left, had anything to say about what to do about the world's foremost terrorist, Osama bin Laden. The Left had no ideas. The consequence of all this was that perspectives and polemics that were borderline before 9/11 suddenly became "mainstream." Minor, marginal or even obscure "progressive" personalities dominated much of the public debates about Islamism, Israel, terrorism and Afghanistan. But the key authority figure above them all was Noam Chomsky.

Back in the early 1980s when I lived in the Annex, the area near the University of Toronto just north of Bloor Street between Spadina and Bathurst, Noam Chomsky was my intellectual hero. You could say he was the hero of the Annex, too. It was a great neighbourhood with a terrific repertory cinema, fine restaurants, Honest Ed's Warehouse for cheap shopping, and three great bookstores within walking distance of my third-floor apartment in one of those red-brick houses.

The SCM bookstore was my favourite. It was started by the Student Christian Movement, a radical ecumenical movement, so it had a huge peace section. Chomsky's titles were usually on offer, and I particularly loved reading Chomsky when I was high on pot. It meant I could never read more than three or four pages at a time, but it was always a revelation. His trick of transposing newspaper headlines and text between Pravda and the New York Times was pretty clever; but when you're giddy from marijuana, it was very, very deep, indeed.

Twenty years later, Chomsky visited the Annex, packing more than 1,000 people into the Bloor Street United Church in November 2002. North Korea, Iraq and Iran were getting a bad rap, because "the real axis of evil is the United States, Israel and Turkey," Chomsky explained. An amusing report about Chomsky's visit, from Toronto's NOW magazine, described a pre-speech reception in his honour at "a lovely Annex home" with "lavish" food and a "shining cluster of Toronto's left intelligentsia," the Toronto Star columnists Linda McQuaig and Rick "The CIA armed and trained bin Laden" Salutin.

During his speech at the church, Chomsky raised the spectre of an Israeli plot to "dismember Iran and reorganize the entire Middle East. . . to reorganize the whole region, expanding the Jordan kingdom to Iraq and Saudi Arabia — a kind of Ottomanization of the region — with the central power in Jerusalem, and the U.S. running the show with regional authority given to parts." The strategy was of crucial importance to radical Bush administration insiders, Chomsky said, because they envisioned unilateral global world domination enforced by absolute American military superiority.

This then was the sort of "analysis" that framed the public debates and controlled the narrative of the liberal intelligentsia in the early years of the decade.

The weirdness wasn't coming from just the Chomskyite Left, either.

Prime Minister Jean Chretien, in an interview with the CBC on the first anniversary of 9/11, seemed to blame the attacks on America. "You cannot exercise your powers to the point of humiliation for the others. That is what the Western world — not only the Americans, the Western world — has to realize. Because they are human beings too. There are long-term consequences." Chretien's point certainly wasn't completely out of line. But some of his Members of Parliament went off the rails, and were applauded for doing so.

For example, Liberal MP Carolyn Parrish, who had earlier complained to the Egyptian newspaper Al-Ahram about the "influence of the Jewish lobby" in Canada, came out of a meeting in February 2003 muttering "Damn Americans, I hate those bastards." In the Toronto Globe and Mail, columnist Heather Mallick wrote that Parrish made Liberals "sound like the party of Lester B. Pearson. We approved." David Collinette, the Minister of Transportation, compared the U.S. to a hockey bully: "There will be people in the U.S. emboldened by their new source of unfettered power to, in a hockey term, get their elbows up."

Over at the Canadian Broadcasting Corporation (CBC) there was a debate over whether and when to use the word "terrorist." CBC News Editor-in-chief Tony Burman (who would go on to take up a senior post at Al-Jazeera, a Qatar-based and government financed version of CNN that is sympathetic to Hamas and notoriously hostile to Israel) explained in a Jan. 2, 2003, article in the Ottawa Citizen that the CBC had settled on a policy of using the words "terrorist" and "terrorism" in its coverage of events in Israel and the rest of the Middle East only when it was unavoidable — when somebody being quoted was actually using the words.

That was the tone of politics at the time. For the Canadian Left, it was all anti-war demonstrations, marches and protests, all the time. StopWar, ANSWER, Not in My Name, Stop the War Coalition, Code Pink, the Canadian Peace Alliance and a host of other organizations rallied in the streets. And the rallies were huge. In March of 2003, on the eve of the U.S.-led invasion of Iraq, roughly 200,000 people turned out for a march in Montreal and 10,000 people marched in Vancouver.

I was at the Marriott World Center Hotel in Orlando, Florida when the war began. It was March 19, 2003. I was there for the annual convention of the National Association of Recording Merchandisers (NARM) and a bunch of us had gathered in the Big Daddy suite. Big Daddy was the American distributor for my record label, NorthernBlues Music. We'd skipped out on the last portion of the awards night. Big Daddy had been passed over for the best small distributor award and Big Daddy's Burt Goldstein and Doug Bail were bummed out. We'd skipped dessert, too. Burt ordered up some ice cream from room service and we all sat around to watch the war's opening act on CNN.

It wasn't anything like 9/11, which had come out of the blue. It was Shock and Awe, baby! How many times do you sit back with your friends, have some ice cream, and watch a war? The Americans were trying to kill Saddam Hussein by bombing his supposed hideouts, and we watched and we watched, hoping Wolf Blitzer or someone would announce the good news — that they'd got him — and maybe the war would end quickly. But it was not to be. Shock and Awe didn't live up to its billing. It was a great television spectacle, but it would take another nine months before the Iraqi dictator was pulled out of a hole in the ground in the town of Ad-Dawr, near Tikrit.

We all went back to our rooms.

I was at the NARM convention to pitch the latest NorthernBlues records. It had been almost two years to the day that I'd shipped my first CDs, and I'd gone on to sign several American and Canadian blues artists. NorthernBlues had an inventory of 15 CDs in total, and in its second year, the company's revenues had already hit $600,000. The CDs I was pitching in Orlando were two very big projects. One was Johnny's Blues, a tribute to my hero Johnny Cash, and the other was Beautiful, the first-ever tribute to Canadian legend Gordon Lightfoot.

Johnny's Blues was a labour of love — it allowed me to reach out to some of my favourite blues artists and have them re-imagine a Johnny Cash song in a blues style. It was a very expensive project for a small record label. Every artist got a $3,000 advance on royalties for each track. My producer, Colin Linden, mastered the project in New York. I'd signed some really great artists, including Gatemouth Brown, Maria Muldaur, Garland Jeffreys, Blackie & The Rodeo Kings, Alvin Youngblood Hart, and Harry Manx.

Beautiful was a collaboration with the Canadian folk music company I'd invested in, Borealis Records. The record was scheduled to be released in September 2003, and we'd managed to sign up some of the biggest names in Canada, including Blue Rodeo, the Cowboy Junkies, the Tragically Hip, Bruce Cockburn, and Ron Sexsmith.

I needed these projects badly, just to keep the bad news off my mind.

There were 40 suicide bombings in Israel in 2001, mostly carried out by Hamas and Palestinian Islamic Jihad — two Islamist terrorist groups dedicated to Israel's destruction. The Dolphinarium discotheque bombing on June 1 killed 21 Israeli teenagers. On Aug. 9 the Sbarro restaurant in Jerusalem was hit and 15 people were killed, including seven children. On Dec. 1, two suicide bombers blew themselves up on Ben Yehuda Street in Jerusalem, a car bomb exploded just as paramedics arrived, and the death toll was 13 with 188 people injured. The very next day, the Haifa 16 bus exploded. Fifteen people were killed and 40 people were injured.

Between Hamas and Palestinian Islamic Jihad, Hamas was the most lethal entity. A Muslim Brotherhood offshoot founded in 1987, Hamas asserts that the Jews were behind the French Revolution and the Bolshevik Revolution, World War I and the destruction of the Ottoman Islamic caliphate, and World War II, and that Israel controls the United States. The Hamas charter also cites the Protocols of the Learned Elders of Zion, a 19th-century fabrication that claims to be the minutes of a Jewish cabal that was conspiring to control the world. The Hamas charter doesn't just call for the destruction of Israel. It calls for the murder of Jews.

In 2002, things got worse. In January, the Israelis intercepted the freighter MV Karine A with 50 tons of weapons, most likely from Iran. On March 2 in Jerusalem a bomb blew up a yeshiva, a religious school, during a bar mitzvah. Eleven people were killed, including two infants and three children. This attack was different. It was carried out by the al-Aqsa Martyrs' Brigade, the terrorist arm of Fatah, and thus directly answerable to Palestinian Liberation Organization leader Yasser Arafat, who had been the supposed Palestinian partner for peace at the July 2000 Camp David Summit. On March 9, a Hamas suicide bomber blew himself up at a coffee shop in Jerusalem killing 11, and on March 27 Hamas attacked a Passover Seder in Netanya, killing 30 people and injuring 140.

Two days after the Netanya attack, Prime Minister Ariel Sharon launched Operation "Defensive Shield," which involved a siege around Arafat's compound in Ramallah and the April 2 Jenin operation that had sparked wild rumours of a massacre. The Jenin operation resulted in the deaths of 23 Israeli soldiers, 22 Palestinian civilians and 30 Palestinian fighters.

When senior PLO official Saeb Erekat claimed more than 500 Palestinians had been slaughtered, mass protests broke out everywhere. North American campuses erupted. Jewish students were beginning to feel threatened. In Montreal, the Concordia University Students Union's *Uprising* magazine claimed that Israel was engaged in "state terror," slaughtering men, women and children "whose only 'crime' is their nationality."

I loved Israel, and I was sick to see this happen. I had spent six months in Israel in 1984. About half that time I lived with a gay friend in Jerusalem. Ran was from India and he had written the first Indian cookbook in Hebrew, using local Israeli ingredients. I spent the next three months on a socialist kibbutz north of Tel Aviv, enrolled in Hebrew classes. We worked half the day and went to school the other half and partied a lot at night. It was great. There were Jews from all over the world — from the U.S., Canada, Brazil, South Africa, Chile, and all over Europe. What was really interesting about the kibbutz was it was home to a Japanese Christian sect, the Makuyas, who believe they have to read the bible in Hebrew. They built a prayer cave on the kibbutz and had their own dormitory. I still smile when I remember travelling on a bus to Jerusalem with a bunch of Japanese people singing Hava Nagila.

During those terrible times after 9/11, during the Second Intifada, social gatherings were becoming more awkward all the time in Ottawa. Almost all my friends were lefties, and it wasn't just the subject of Israel that was making dinner parties uncomfortable. It was also George Bush's war to depose Saddam Hussein.

At the time, I thought the decision to invade Iraq and remove Saddam was the right thing to do. Donald Rumsfeld made a complete mess of it, and the Americans had made too much of the suspicion that Saddam possessed WMDs. But there was a good case for the overthrow of the regime.

Saddam Hussein was no ordinary dictator. He'd started two wars — against Iran in 1980, and in 1990 he annexed Kuwait. He'd waged a genocidal war against the Kurds, with mass executions and chemical weapons. In just one afternoon, he killed 5,000 Kurdish people by poison gas at Halabja. In all, Saddam killed more than 180,000 Kurds and destroyed over 2,000 Kurdish villages. After his army was chased out of Kuwait, he executed between 60,000 and 130,000 Shiites. His secret police used to hang dissidents from meat hooks. He also hosted a variety of terrorist leaders — Abu Abbas, Abu Nidal, Carlos the Jackal — and several terrorist organizations. Abdul Rahman Yasin, who prepared the bombs for the first World Trade Center attack in 1993, lived in Baghdad until the 2003 invasion. Abu Mussab al-Zarqawi, the head of Al-Qaida in Iraq, moved there from Afghanistan right after 9/11. Saddam also routinely rewarded the families of Palestinian suicide bombers with cash payments of $25,000 per suicide bomber.

And it wasn't just the Bush administration that believed Saddam possessed weapons of mass destruction. At least a dozen intelligence agencies around the world put his possession of WMDs as a high probability. Immediately before the war, Jordan's King Abdullah told U.S. General Tommy Franks that the Iraqis possessed both biological and chemical weapons. Hosni Mubarak, the president of Egypt, also told Franks: "We have spoken with Saddam Hussein. He is a madman. He has weapons of mass destruction, biological weapons." Top officials in President Bill Clinton's administration had also been convinced. In July of 2003, Clinton said that when he left office in January 2001, he was convinced Saddam possessed "a substantial amount of biological and chemical material" that was unaccounted for. And Clinton signed the Iraq Liberation Act in 1998, which committed the United States to a policy of "regime change." For more than a decade before the 2003 invasion, the U.S., the U.K. and France were enforcing U.N. Security Council-authorized no-fly zones to protect the Kurdish population in the north and the Shiite population in the south. Hardly a day went by without anti-aircraft fire from Iraqi artillery. One could hardly call this a peaceful situation.

Some people, like Prime Minister Chretien, said that Saddam was "contained" and that he posed little threat. But the sanctions regime was leaking: the regime was evading UN sanctions by trading oil that was supposed to be used for food. Saddam was building palaces and bribing UN officials, earning an estimated $11 billion from illegal trading.

Right or wrong, the United States went to war, and within three weeks the regime fell. It can't be denied that the majority of Iraqis were quite happy to see him go, and not just the joyous and celebrating Kurds. There were any number of things about the invasion that were worth debating, but instead of a vigorous debate, something like derangement was sweeping through the culture. The CBC's struggle with coherence on the subject of the word "terrorism" was part of that. In the broadly left-wing community where my own values were nurtured, something like dementia was setting in, and anti-Israel polemics and anti-Semitic messaging started to show up at rallies that had nothing to do with Israel, at least outwardly.

In February 2003, at an "anti-war" rally in Victoria, B.C. somebody brought along a sign referring to a "Jewish worldwide conspiracy." The following month in Toronto, at a combined "anti-poverty" and "anti-war" rally, a demonstrator insisted that Jews participating in the rally should go home. Indymedia, a worldwide activist website that emerged in the run-up to the 1999 anti-globalization riots in Seattle, was like an asylum. The web network became a gathering place for anti-capitalist conspiracy theorists obsessed with Israel and with Jews. In May 2002, Indymedia's Hamilton and Windsor editions featured The Hidden Tyranny, a 1976 tract purporting to be an interview with a Harold Rosenthal, "an influential Jew learned in Jewish ways" who was intimately familiar with "the invisible world of Jewry." The document was an amateurish recapitulation of the Protocols of Zion.

Not long after Iraq invasion, "anti-war" coalitions and their various (ostensibly) left-wing parties and activist fronts had almost invariably morphed into co-ventures and collaborations with virulently anti-Israel groups, most notably of the far-right, Islamist kind — sometimes Sunni-derived, sometimes Khomeinist.

The foundation of these alliances was solidified in the lead-up to the Iraq war at the first of several annual conferences in Cairo that brought together hundreds of Canadian, American and European activists. The founding conference in 2002 was organized by the Egyptian Popular Campaign to Confront U.S. Aggression, uniting "anti-war" and anti-globalization activists with several Islamist, Baathist and militant Palestinian groups. Delegates approved a declaration blasting "Zionist perpetrators of genocidal crimes against the Palestinian people," and the "power asymmetry of the existing world order." Its to-do list included sending "human shields" to Iraq, forming anti-Israel solidarity committees to support the Palestinian right to "resistance and struggle" and organizing boycotts of "U.S. and Israeli commodities."

Signatories to the first Cairo declaration were not merely marginal and frustrated Marxist college dropouts. Among them: George Galloway, the "maverick" British MP who would go on to be kicked out of the Labour Party for inciting Arabs to fight British troops, and for urging British troops to disobey orders; prominent playwright and screenwriter Harold Pinter, who would go on to such awards and honours as a Nobel Prize and his investiture as a Commander of the British Empire and the

French Legion d'honneur; the popular environmentalist and Guardian columnist George Monbiot; fabulously successful movie maker and film director Ken Loach, recipient of several honorary doctorates; actor Julie Christie; writer Tariq Ali; and Ali Mallah, vice president of the Canadian Arab Federation and vice president of the Ontario New Democratic Party.

About 800 attendees showed up for the 2003 conference, which brought together "anti-war" leaders and icons such as former U.S. President Lyndon Johnson's attorney general, the eccentric Ramsay Clark, with Ma'mun al-Hodeiby, leader of Egypt's semi-outlawed Muslim Brotherhood and a delegation from Saddam Hussein's deposed government in Baghdad. The conference melded resistance to "capitalist globalization and U.S. hegemony" with the "heroic Palestinian intifada against the Occupation" and "Iraqi resistance to Occupation." The point was to form a "unified front against imperialist and capitalist globalization." To that end, the conference pledged support for Palestinian militants' rejection of the Oslo peace accords, and committed delegates to persist in "refusing normalization with the Zionist entity in all fields" and to "mobilize so that the UN readopts its resolution equating Zionism with racism."

In Canada, the most extreme, far-right Islamists and anti-Israel terrorist groups were embraced by "pacifists" and "anti-war" activists. One of the most prominent figures to emerge as a spokesman of the Toronto Stop the War Coalition was Zafar Bangash from the Institute of Contemporary Islamic Thought (ICIT), a Khomeinist think-tank in service of Tehran's ruling ayatollahs. In 2003, when the Liberal Canadian government added the Palestine Liberation Front (PLF), the Popular Front for the Liberation of Palestine (PFLP) and the PFLP General Command to its list of terrorist entities, Vancouver's Stop War coalition joined with several activist and "pro-Palestinian" groups to protest the decision on the grounds that it was "going down the path of McCarthyism at home." Among the PLF's many atrocities, the best known was its 1985 hijacking of the cruise ship Achille Lauro, when the elderly wheelchair-bound American tourist Leon Klinghoffer was shot in the head and thrown overboard. The PFLP hijacked three airliners in the 1970s and killed an Israeli cabinet member in 2001. The PFLP-GC, meanwhile, was the first Palestinian organization to use suicide bombers. The Stop War complainants attacked Ottawa's decision as "support for Israeli aggression, occupation and injustice against the Palestinian, Arab and Muslim people" and warned that Ottawa was taking a path that would "endanger the strategic interests of the Canadian people for generations to come."

The activists from the Cairo conferences continued their work in Canada, and their efforts were by no means confined to speeches delivered in the basements of out-of-the-way labour halls. By November 2005, the West Block of Parliament Hill in Ottawa was the venue for a multi-seminar conference titled "Challenging Canada's Role in Empire." The conference sponsors included the Canadian Peace Alliance (associated with the "Respect Party" of disgraced British MP and Cairo conventioneer George Galloway), Muslim Presence Ottawa, and other groups of the far-left, "anti-imperialist" variety. Speakers at the three-day conference included Ali Mallah of the Canadian Arab Federation (the CAF would go on to lose its federal funding over its apparent links to terrorist and anti-Semitic groups) and the Khomeinist ICIT propagandist Zafar Bangash — a 9/11 conspiracy theorist of the "they let it happen" school.

Adbusters was a lavishly produced Vancouver-based "anti-capitalist" journal with a worldwide circulation of 40,000. Its stable of contributing writers matched that of any glossy "capitalist" American magazine. The March 2004 issue contained an article listing all the "neoconservatives" in the Bush administration, with the Jewish names highlighted. Adbusters' publisher Kelle Lasn, the article's author, claimed that "some commentators are worried that these individuals — labelled 'Likudniks' for their links to Israel's right wing Likud party — do not distinguish between American and Israeli interests. For example, whose interests were they protecting in pushing for war in Iraq?"

All hell broke loose during the visit of President Bush to Ottawa in December of 2004. A Globe and Mail article captured the insanity of the time by noting that "a coalition of anti-war protesters, left-wing lawyers and anti-capitalists refused yesterday to condemn those who might resort to violence" during his visit. Thomas Walkom of the Toronto Star wrote on Nov. 16 that Bush "was a perfect candidate for prosecution under Canada's Crimes against Humanity and War Crimes Act." Elizabeth May, the executive director of the Sierra Club of Canada (and later the leader of the Green Party), wrote: "Bush represents death. We call on Canadians to greet him by tying black crepe or cloth ribbons to everything in sight." Carolyn "Damn Americans" Parrish was at it again, stomping on a Bush doll on CBC. A dozen protestors were arrested outside the Museum of Civilization where Bush attended a dinner in his honour.

To get a sense of the hysterical tenor of the time, one just has to read through the columns of the Toronto Star's Haroon Siddiqui. The Toronto Star was no ordinary newspaper — its weekly circulation, at 3.26 million, was half again bigger than its nearest competitor, the Globe and Mail. And Siddiqui was not some marginal opinion writer. He was also the Toronto Star's Editorial Page Editor Emeritus, and a leading figure of the Canadian liberal establishment. After emigrating to Canada from India at the suggestion of Roland Michener, no less — Michener was the Canadian High Commissioner to India in the late 1960s, and was later Governor-General — Siddiqui would go on to be awarded an Order of Canada, an Order of Ontario, an honorary Doctor of Letters from York University, a membership in the board of the Canadian Club and the advisory board of the Ryerson University School of Journalism.

In Siddiqui's Toronto Star columns, Canada was always in immediate peril of war-mongering American subterfuge, always just inches away from being conned into enlistment in neoconservative American wars on Muslims. George W. Bush was "a hostage to hawks at home and in Israel," Israel was always the bad guy and Arabs the innocent victim. The Khomeinist regime is dependably sophisticated and moderate.

Just about any crank with an anti-American conspiracy theory and any Third World strongman obsessed with Israel would sooner or later appear, favourably, in one of Siddiqui's columns.

Three months after 9/11, Siddiqui wrote that Osama bin Laden "was trained by the CIA." Siddiqui was back with an Islamist conspiracy-theory falsehood less than a year later when he wrote in September 2002 that the civil liberties of American Muslims had been "suspended post-Sept. 11." In the same conspiracy-theory realm, Siddiqui asserted in June 2003 that American foreign policy under George Bush was a matter of "a born-again Christian, who also happens to be presiding over history's biggest military apparatus" venturing forth on "a holy mission." In September 2003, Siddiqui wrote: "Syria is accused, as was Iraq, of developing chemical and biological weapons." The U.S. was similarly mistreating Iran with accusations of "harbouring terrorists." But Syria was known to be actively undertaking a covert nuclear program and a chemical-weapons program at the time, and Iran was openly an active sponsor, arms-supplier and funder of Hezbollah and other terrorist groups.

In Siddiqui's world, the mere acknowledgement of these facts was to be duped by the propaganda tricks employed by a neoconservative "cabal" within the Bush administration (oddly, however, "the Arab Middle East" was happy with the Bush Republican's defeat of Al Gore, Siddiqui wrote, because Gore was "backed by an overwhelming number of Jewish-American voters"). When good guys showed up among the invariably American and Israeli bad guys in Siddiqui's columns, they were usually found in the Khomeinist regime in Tehran and its proxies.

In December 2001, Siddiqui wrote that Khomeinist Iran "has produced an elected class of moderates who are leading the intellectual debate on democracy in the Muslim world." American claims about the Khomeinists' meddling in Afghanistan and its harbouring of Al-Qaida terrorists were "spurious," Siddiqui claimed in February 2002 (in fact, both claims were incontrovertibly true). The Americans should not be believed when they talk about the brutal repression Iranians were suffering under the ayatollahs because what really bothered the United States was the Khomeinist regime's "history of unapologetic support for those resisting Israeli occupation, in southern Lebanon and now the occupied territories," meaning Hezbollah and Hamas.

Siddiqui wasn't the only Toronto Star luminary writing along these lines. Linda McQuaig wrote more than 150 columns for the Star from 2001 to 2005. Some of her columns' headlines: "Linda McQuaig says moving closer to US promotes war, not peacemaking;" "Linda McQuaig says today's charade is simply about Iraq's oil; history will show US lusted after oil;" "Bush sells sizzle in war on terror;" "Pliable Bush puppet of hawks;" "Rebuffed President recklessly saddles up for war;" "The Thing is, it is about oil;" "U.S. wants to liberate our energy;" "Africa suffers, West chants mantra of trade, not aid."

McQuaig also appeared regularly in Rabble.ca, a webzine founded in April 2001 by activist Judy Rebick and others to provide "a needed space for issues, a place to explore political passions and an opportunity to expand ideas." A former president of the National Action Committee on the Status of Women, Rebick was a longtime NDP activist and a leader (along with MPs Libby Davies and Svend Robinson) of the New Politics Initiative, which aimed to move the NDP further to the left. Rabble provided a platform for left-wing writers like Rick Salutin, Naomi Klein and Murray Dobbin, and also regularly linked to commentaries from The Guardian, Edward Said, Znet, Noam Chomsky, Robert Fisk, John Pilger, Alexander Cockburn and others of that sort.

After 9/11, Rabble saw its unique visitors rise from 38,000 to 50,000 a month. Other "progressive sites" also enjoyed huge spikes in readership. The Nation went from 65,000 a day to more than 100,000. Zmag, the home of Noam Chomsky, saw its traffic more than triple to 200,000 visitors per week. People were clearly anxious for "alternative" explanations for the new era 9/11 had ushered in, but in Canada, you didn't have to go to "alternative" sites to find them. Rabble columnists routinely showed up in the mainstream media — the Toronto Star, the Globe and Mail and the CBC — and vice-versa. Rick Salutin wrote weekly for the Globe and Mail. Linda McQuaig wrote regularly for the Toronto Star. Naomi Klein found an international home in the Nation, and a domestic home at the Globe and Mail. Judy Rebick wrote occasionally for the Star, and was a regular guest on the CBC. Maude Barlow and Gerald Caplan, who also wrote regularly for Rabble, started showing up in the Toronto Star and the Globe and Mail.

The Rabble writer whose columns seemed to move most seamlessly between the Globe and Mail, the CBC and the Toronto Star was Heather Mallick, who lamented in a September 2003 Globe column that "Iraq's 23 million people are now enslaved by Texans." To Mallick, George W. Bush was a war criminal, and when Bush came to Ottawa, Mallick argued that Canadian authorities should take the opportunity to arrest him. But Canada was already succumbing to the Bush administration's domineering, out of fear of incurring American wrath, Mallick wrote: "The only question is how precisely the Bush cult, one of the most violent on Earth led by a self-declared 'war president' will try to humiliate us."

What could have been legitimate protest against the Iraq war had morphed into total incoherence. Americans were now as evil, or more evil, than Al-Qaida. The Iraqi people were now enslaved by a war over oil. Suicide bombing was a legitimate tactic to oppose Israel. George Bush and Dick Cheney were war criminals who needed to be brought to justice, and as for Islamist terrorism, we just needed to understand the root causes.

At a gay dinner party in Ottawa, I ended up in a nasty argument after being asked a question that was making the rounds a lot in those days: Why should the Palestinians suffer because of the Holocaust? It was a particularly horrible conversation because it was really about whether Israel even had a right to exist. I was told I was "right wing," which was amusing, since I'd been a critic of Israel's settlement policy ever since my early lefty days in the 1970s. I'd always supported a Palestinian state. I did then, and I still do.

More email fights ensued. I was losing more friends. I was loathe to go to dinner parties —everybody would be denouncing George Bush and saying stupid things about Americans. And I really didn't need more people to tell me how Israel was the cause of all evil.

It was time to go elsewhere and find new places to hang out.

Three

A New Home

On a warm evening in May 2005, I found myself walking into the Centretown Pub, a very popular gay bar in Ottawa, with a tall and boyishly handsome 40-year-old man. Keith Fountain was his name. I'd met him at a coffee shop a few months earlier, and we'd hit it off right away.

Keith was a diplomat, on leave from Foreign Affairs. He'd been posted to Pakistan, Poland and Malaysia. He'd opened Canada's embassy in Afghanistan. Our views of the world were similar enough that I could count on conversations with him not degenerating into arguments about Israel or George Bush, and that sure was a nice change. Keith was very, very smart, too.

But we weren't on a date. Keith was married with one daughter. He was the Conservative Party candidate in Ottawa Centre. I'd just been appointed his director of communications by my fellow members of the Conservative Party of Canada's Ottawa Centre Electoral District Association (EDA).

The last time I'd been involved in anything remotely political in Ottawa was more than 20 years before, when I was on the organizing committee of an anti-war mobilization that brought 15,000 protestors to Parliament Hill to protest Canada's cooperation with U.S. President Ronald Reagan's cruise missile program. And yet here I was, making the rounds with Ottawa Centre's Conservative candidate, drumming up support for him in the coming election, whenever that was going to be. That seems like quite the change. But maybe not so much.

It had all started with a chance meeting with a university student,

Kristin Baldwin, at a "small c" conservative luncheon in town. While we were chatting during a break, she mentioned that she was working for Fountain. I'd told her that I had a hard time with Conservatives, mostly because of their opposition to same-sex marriage. Kristin suggested I should meet Keith. He was in favour of a same-sex marriage law. So I gave her my card. I got an email from Keith, and we met for coffee.

Keith wasn't in any way what I'd expected of a Conservative Party guy. He was very "socially liberal," supporting same-sex marriage, a woman's right to choose, and the legalization of marijuana. He was fiscally conservative, though, which was also fine by me. I liked him. The next thing I knew I was not only a member of the Conservative Party, but a party activist.

At the Centretown Pub, Keith and I went from table to table, talking to people. We were received quite warmly. It helped that Keith was a same-sex marriage supporter, but most people wanted to talk about taxation, health care, honest government and a variety of other issues. It certainly didn't hurt that Keith was handsome and had a great smile — this was a gay bar, after all — and he certainly didn't look like the stereotypical Conservative Party candidate.

When we were finished making the rounds, we sat down to have a beer and Keith was happy. Despite what you might think from reading the gay media, gay people worry about most of the same issues that straight people do. Gay people pay the same taxes and face the same challenges as everybody else. It was clear that the Conservatives could get gay voters, at least in Ottawa Centre, and any hostility people had towards the Conservative Party tended to melt away when people met Keith.

For me, joining a political party, let alone the Conservative Party, was definitely a new and strange experience. I'd always been wary of political parties because of their tendency to demand rigid and unwavering ideological support from party members, and their intolerance for differing political opinions in the rank and file. In my early days, I'd never entertained the idea of joining the NDP. I'd considered the NDP too wishy-washy — and too conservative for my taste. I figured I'd just end up arguing with my fellow party members. In my activism I always felt I could get more done outside the party system.

Even after I joined the Conservatives, I was still highly sceptical of the party, particularly because of what I'd heard about the strength of the party's "social conservative" wing. But I figured that some kindred spirits might find their way to the Keith Fountain campaign, and it was a way for me to move into a completely different social milieu and to make some new friends. I'd been avoiding all those social occasions where politics would come up. Hardly anybody in my circles seemed capable of engaging in rational discussions about real issues anymore. I was finding myself in interminable arguments.

I'd even become loathe to check my emails. My most sensible and even non-political friends, people I'd known since my university days, seemed to want to talk about nothing except how stupid George Bush was, how the Americans were obese warmongers, how Palestine and Iran were no less democratic than the United States — that kind of thing. How does one even respond to emails like that?

I dreaded going to parties because I knew if I said anything, I'd be the lone voice on any number of topics. When a party turned into a loud chorus of George Bush denunciations — this happened a lot — my choice was to either stay silent or say something nobody wanted to hear and get myself labelled as someone who just liked to argue. But staying silent just made me angry. It was a bit like the days when I was "in the closet," so coming out as a Conservative in 2005 was an experience a bit like coming out as gay in 1983, when I was 26. I'd been a bit of a "late bloomer" back then, too.

Not long after I joined the Conservative Party and went to work on Fountain's campaign, I had lunch with my old friend Peggy Berkowitz, the very first friend I'd "come out" to as a gay man back in my activist days in the Annex. Peggy and I had worked together for the Georgian, the student newspaper at the Sir George Williams campus of Concordia in Montreal. After I'd moved to Toronto and started dating men,

I realized I had to come out to my friends. But where was I to start? Who do I tell first? I'd chosen Peggy. I'd felt she'd be the most open and empathetic, and she was.

Peggy's cousin Arlene had married the famous abortion-rights crusader Henry Morgentaler, and when Peggy and Gerry Toomey got married I sat at the same table as Henry and his son at the wedding reception. We had a wonderful time. Gerry had ended up being one of the only people in my left-wing circles that I could have a civil conversation with in the days after 9/11 (Gerry was the guy whose main concern was whether warfare in Afghanistan would disrupt UN food aid supplies). By 1983, Peggy was writing for the Wall Street Journal, and we'd rekindled our friendship when she moved to Toronto. Coming out to her — to anyone — required courage.

Coming out was still a very big deal in 1983, and when I called Peggy on the telephone, my hands were shaking. We planned a get-together over dinner, which gave me a few days to prepare myself. Over dinner, I took quite some time to broach the subject. I was expecting the worst. Peggy reacted with surprise, but then, okay, no problem, let's move on. An enormous weight was lifted from my shoulders. Coming out to the rest of my friends turned out to be easy. Nobody reacted badly. Coming out as a Conservative more than 20 years later proved to be a much bigger deal.

When I met with Peggy for lunch in April 2005, the controversial, polarizing feminist Andrea Dworkin had just died — I was in the camp that considered Dworkin a man-hater — and Peggy started right in on that. She spent half the lunch arguing in defence of Dworkin and her politics. This just drummed home why I'd reached out to the Conservatives — which was something Peggy just couldn't understand. I talked to her about Keith Fountain. It made no difference. Nothing I said made any difference. Apart from Gerry Toomey — by that time he and Peggy had divorced — it was the same with all my other left-wing friends. It was either the subject that was not to be discussed, or a subject of argument.

Even though I was still extremely busy with NorthernBlues, I was spending all my spare time working on the Fountain campaign. It had gone from coffee with Keith to being in charge of working with the press in about five minutes — it had happened that fast. I barely had any time to take it all in. I knew I wasn't going to be able to support everything about the Conservatives and I knew I'd have to deal with people I'd disagree with — about same-sex marriage, homosexuality, abortion and a host of other issues. But I felt I had to go down that path to see where it went.

From the start, everybody I met in Fountain's campaign, and on the Conservative EDA board, was terrific. People were supportive of Israel. They were against "political correctness." There was very little anti-Americanism. You could say something nice about George Bush and nobody was going to recoil. And nobody batted an eye about me being gay. If it bothered anyone, I certainly didn't notice.

It was a new home. At least for now. And God knows, I needed a new home.

It was bad enough that so many of my old friends seemed to have become irrational. What was worse was that it was as though everyone had become fervent disciples of the American filmmaker Michael Moore, the clown-prince of the Left's new irrational politics. In Canada at the time, you couldn't be a sentient being without bumping into Michael Moore: his films, his books, his appearances on talk shows, his interviews in the newspapers.

Moore was huge in the United States, but he was obsessed with Canada. In *Bowling for Columbine*, his 1995 Hollywood feature film *Canadian Bacon*, his television series *TV Nation*, Moore was constantly playing the stereotype of the peace-loving, intelligent Canadian as a foil against the stereotypical gun-happy warmongering American. Canadians returned the favour by being obsessed with him. Moore's *Fahrenheit 9/11* was in all the first-run cinemas, the repertory theatres and all over North American campuses. He was a fixture on *Larry King Live* on CNN. But he was a favourite of almost every CBC show you could name, his books were bestsellers in Canada and he dominated the culture in a way that was quite unlike anybody else. When he launched his book *Stupid White Men*, he told the Toronto Star that in just two days, he'd gotten more intense media interest in Canada than at any time during his U.S. book tour.

Because Moore was such a hero to so many Canadians, it's worthwhile taking a moment to have a look at the phenomenon. It is a rich and telling illustration of everything that has gone wrong with the Left, particularly in Canada, and with the broadly liberal cultural milieu that was so dominant in Canada in the years after Sept. 11, 2001.

When *Fahrenheit 9/11* opened in cinemas across Canada, the Toronto Star's Geoff Pevere swooned. He wrote that the "convincingly argued" point of Moore's film was that the Bush family was "politically compromised" because of the family's interests in oil industry. The war in Iraq was a result of that compromise, and Sept. 11th had provided the excuse "to secure and protect" the Bush family's interests. Toronto Star editor emeritus and columnist Haroon Siddiqui was similarly impressed, crediting Moore with forcing Americans to undergo "a major political rethink". This was, you could say, the "establishment view" of Moore in Canada. The approval Moore got from Pevere and Siddiqui wasn't particularly exceptional. It was typical.

During his remarks to the Toronto Star before the *Fahrenheit 9/11* Canadian premiere in Toronto on June 18, 2004, Moore said his hope was that his film would help prevent Conservative leader Stephen Harper from becoming prime minister. "I hope this doesn't happen. Bush is going to throw a party. He's going to be a happy man. (Harper) has a big pair of scissors in his hand. He wants to snip away at your social safety net. He'd like this to be the 51st state." What he wanted Canadians to take away from his film was that a Harper victory would mean getting drawn into the war in Iraq: "Get ready to send your kids over to die for nothing, so that Bush's buddies can line their pockets."

Fahrenheit 9/11 was based on these claims: Bush stole the 2000 presidential election from Al Gore with help from his brother, Florida

Governor Jeb Bush; American foreign policy is run for the Saudis, who own seven per cent of the U.S. economy; the Afghanistan intervention was purely for Saudi business interests; George Bush, because he was governor of Texas at the time, had been involved with talks between the Unocal company and the Taliban about a proposed gas pipeline through Afghanistan; the Bush administration allowed the bin Laden family to leave the U.S. immediately after 9/11, before they were vetted. The film also depicted Saddam Hussein's Iraq as a happy place before 9/11 and a country that was not a threat to the United States.

None of these things was true.

Bush didn't steal the troubled Florida election, with or without his brother Jeb's help. The vote was essentially tied in Florida given the margin of error of the voting machines. However, two major media investigations, one by USA Today, the Miami Herald and Knight-Ridder, and the other by the Associated Press, the Wall Street Journal, CNN and the New York Times, looked into Florida's tight-race confusion, and found that Bush beat Gore, even by the recount standards set by the Gore campaign. The U.S.-led intervention in Afghanistan had nothing to do with Saudi interests. The Saudis didn't own anything like seven per cent of the U.S. economy — Saudi money made up about seven per cent of foreign investment in the United States. Unocal's aborted gas pipeline deal with the Taliban arose in 1998, during the Clinton administration, and the Bush family had nothing to do with it. The bin Laden family members departed only after the FBI vetted them and they got no special treatment from the White House. Bush certainly wasn't running foreign policy to favour the Saudis — the Saudis opposed the American invasion of Iraq. Iraq was not a happy place before 9/11. Saddam Hussein's torture chambers and mass graves were scattered throughout the country. Saddam posed a constant threat to the American interests. The Baathist dictator paid millions of dollars to suicide bombers attacking Israel and had even once tried to assassinate former President George H.W. Bush.

Apart from Moore's big lies, there were just as many little lies. But in the liberal-left irrationality that seemed to have taken over in Canada at the time, lies didn't seem to matter anymore. Neither did the truth.

In a column arguing that the cost of the United States' military involvement in Iraq and Afghanistan was borne by poor people, "while rich, private interests benefit," the Toronto Star's Linda McQuaig zeroed in on a scene in *Fahrenheit 9/11* that Moore had fictionalized. Bush appears to be addressing a gala dinner of wealthy supporters, referring to them as "the haves and the have-mores. Some people call you the elite. I call you my base." The dinner was in fact a fundraiser for charity, one of the annual white-tie fundraising affairs convened by the Alfred E. Smith Memorial Foundation at which politicians typically make fun of themselves. Alfred E. Smith was himself a reformist Democrat, a Roman Catholic whose decidedly progressive bid for the U.S. presidency in 1928 was defeated not only by the relative rise in prosperity of the time but also because of a fair amount of anti-Catholic bigotry.

That's just a smattering of the distortions in *Fahrenheit 9/11.*

I first encountered Michael Moore's work in 1989, with his documentary *Roger & Me.* I was deeply moved by it. The film centres on the town of Flint, Michigan, which in 1978 had about 80,000 people working in the automobile industry, but a decade later was devastated by mass layoffs at General Motors. To counter the effects of GM's contraction, the town engaged in a variety of weird schemes that were presented in *Roger & Me* in such a way as to make the audience cringe with embarrassment. Throughout the film, Moore runs after GM CEO Roger Smith (the "Roger" of the documentary's title) for an interview, but gets only a fleeting chance to ask a few questions at the chairman's annual Christmas message in 1988.

It's a very powerful film, but as I would later learn, *Roger & Me* is based on a fiction. Its many deceptions had gone completely unnoticed by the major film critics at the time. As the left-wing Canadian filmmakers Debbie Melnyk and Rick Caine exposed in their own documentary, *Manufacturing Dissent*, in 2007, Moore's determined but failed quest to interview GM's Roger Smith was just a dramatic device, a fabrication. Moore had spoken to Smith on at least two occasions apart from the fleeting encounter Moore depicts in the film. As for Flint's strange marketing tactics, they were well under way long before GM's layoffs, a fact that Moore worked around by reversing the true story's timeframes.

Moore's 2002 documentary *Bowling for Columbine* employed outright lies to build his case that the high rate of violent crime in the United States reflected deep American pathologies on the world stage. The film draws a cause-and-effect connection between the 1999 Columbine school shootings in Columbine, Colorado, which left 12 students and a teacher dead, and a Lockheed Martin plant in nearby Littleton that shows up in the film as a sinister and secretive weapons manufacturing facility.

A key scene in the film presents Moore carrying a free gun out of a bank after opening an account — a nice perk for gun-mad Americans. It was a fabrication. The bank's free gun offer was real, everything else was faked. A scene presenting Canada as a place so much safer than the U.S. that people don't even lock their front doors (filmed in Sarnia, Ontario, every door Moore tries to open is unlocked) was faked. As Melnyk and Caine exposed in *Manufacturing Dissent*, only four of the ten doors Moore tried to open was unlocked (according to a 2008 State Farm Insurance survey, that's roughly the same proportion of Americans who leave their front doors unlocked).

In *Bowling for Columbine's* closing montage, Osama bin Laden is presented as having been trained by the United States during the 1980s (here's that conspiracy theory again), and against the backdrop of the hijacked passenger planes plunging into the Twin Towers, these words appear: "Osama bin Laden uses his expert CIA training to murder 3,000 people."

That we Canadians liked to believe we were better than the Americans — which Michael Moore spent a great part of his career telling us — was one thing. That the Left's beliefs rested on so many lies was what I found so troubling —and worse, that the Left was seemingly unable to face up to the consequences of its own beliefs. It was right to call out the U.S government for saying things that were not true —

lies have consequences. But it was another thing to lie about what the Bush administration really believed about Saddam Hussein's WMDs, by asserting that Bush and his cohorts were simply lying. They were not, as the assessments of so many intelligence agencies around the world, and the conclusions reached by top officials in President Bill Clinton's administration, make clear.

But the Left's lies and the Left's beliefs will have their consequences, too. In the case of Michael Moore and his "anti-war" politics, the polemicist Christopher Hitchens put it this way: "If Michael Moore had had his way, Slobodan Milosevic would still be the big man in a starved and tyrannical Serbia. Bosnia and Kosovo would have been cleansed and annexed. If Michael Moore had been listened to, Afghanistan would still be under Taliban rule, and Kuwait would have remained part of Iraq. And Iraq itself would still be the personal property of a psychopathic crime family, bargaining covertly with the slave state of North Korea for WMD."

To a great many people, these things didn't seem to matter much. Moore's fan base was massive. *Fahrenheit 9/11* took in more than $228 million in ticket sales and more than 3 million DVDs were sold. It was the highest-grossing documentary in history, and it made Moore fabulously rich.

With our cultural arteries clogged up like this, I wanted to do something about it.

My old friend Jeffrey Asher, who'd been a socialist professor of mine at Dawson College in Montreal, wanted to do something too. Like me, Jeffrey had ended up in Ottawa, and started leaning to the conservative side of things around the same time I had (he'd gone much farther to the right than me, as I later learned). Jeffrey had taught the humanities course I took in my first year at Dawson. It was called World Simulation. The class was divided into countries and you had to trade commodities, manage a budget and write strategy papers. You could declare war, even. There was a weekly newspaper to keep everybody up to date on how the game was going. It was a great way to learn about politics and

international affairs. Jeffrey was a socialist and an atheist. By the time I'd
finished his course, so was I.

And there we were, all those years later in Ottawa, cooking up
ideas. Why not start a book club? Maybe we'd find other like-minded
people. We could all read books together and have discussion meetings
about the books. No party politics allowed. So, for lack of a better name,
we called ourselves the Right Book Club of Ottawa, I put a small ad in
the Ottawa Citizen to drum up some interest, and away we went.

Our suggested subject list was a grab bag. Anti-Americanism,
the United Nations and its failures, terrorism, Israel, the psychiatry
industry, men's rights, multiculturalism, media bias, globalization,
environmentalism, libertarianism, capitalism, the Left — things like
that. We even put up flyers in libraries. We managed to attract a core
group of about six people. After a few books, a few meetings over dinner
in restaurants and a lot of bickering — about same-sex marriage, for
instance — the book club was over in about six months. So was my
friendship with Jeffrey.

But just as that little effort was wrapping up, I discovered that
a young American filmmaker, Michael Wilson, had just produced
a documentary called *Michael Moore Hates America*. The film premiered
in 2004. Wilson had turned the table on Moore and chased him all over
the United States, in much the same way that Moore pretended to chase
GM's Roger Smith, only for real. So I got in touch with the Bytowne,
our local repertory cinema, to see if they would bring in the film. They
said they wouldn't — they didn't think it would bring in enough paying
customers — but suggested that maybe I could rent a hall myself and
bring it in.

An interesting idea, for sure. It was an idea I would later pursue, in
a way that would end up taking over my life in a big way.

It was around this time that I discovered Andrew Sullivan, one of
the most prominent gay intellectuals in the United States. Sullivan was
a conservative. He supported Bush on the Iraq War. He supported the
State of Israel. He'd been a longtime supporter of same-sex marriage. I

began to start my day reading Sullivan's hugely popular blog, the Daily Dish. I started reading his books, too. He was a breath of fresh air, and the Daily Dish inspired me to start my own blog.

I launched GayandRight in March 2005, starting out with content that would appeal to Canadian conservatives like me: the UN's bias against Israel; men's rights, the CBC's anti-American biases; Al Jazeera's conspiracy theories; Iran's arming of Hamas in Gaza; and the rise of anti-Semitism in Europe and Canada. I touched on North Korea, Saddam Hussein's "Oil for Palaces" program and the catastrophe in Darfur. I was busy. The day Andrew Sullivan linked to GayandRight I got several thousand hits. I joined Blogging Tories, an aggregator of conservative Canadian blogs, and I put an ad for GayandRight in Ottawa's gay community newspaper. My hit counts went up. I started getting emails from around the world. It was amazing.

I noticed that I was getting three basic types of email. The first type was the angry conservative who said I could be conservative but not gay. The second type was the angry gay man who said I could be gay but not conservative (as though gay people possessed a liberal gene). This second type made me angry. I'd spent a large part of my life fighting for gay rights, our rights to be ourselves, and now gay people were telling me how I should think? The third type was the most interesting: the gay conservative saying, boy, am I happy I found you, I just knew I wasn't alone! I got so many like that I started to think about setting up a gay conservative organization in Canada.

Another interesting idea. It would have to wait for another day, but that idea, like the Bytowne's suggestion that I bring in my own films, would also end up a big part of my life.

Meanwhile, Prime Minister Paul Martin's Liberal minority government collapsed in November and the election was set for Jan. 23, 2006. It went on to be a long campaign — eight weeks — and there was a break in the middle for Christmas and New Year.

I threw myself into Keith Fountain's campaign. It was going to be my job to keep Keith's schedule, distribute it every night to his campaign team, write and distribute press releases, arrange for media interviews and travel with Keith to most of his campaign events. The incumbent MP in Ottawa-Centre was former NDP leader Ed Broadbent, but he'd retired, so the riding's NDP flag was passed to Paul Dewar, an Ottawa school teacher and the son of a former Ottawa mayor. The Liberal was lawyer and lobbyist Richard Mahoney. It was a tough riding, a Liberal stronghold before Broadbent moved into it. Keith had a fair shot at it, though.

I was really looking forward to the campaign, but it got off on a really, really bad note. The Conservative campaign in Ottawa kicked off on Tuesday, Nov. 29, with a rally at Conservative candidate John Baird's Ottawa West – Nepean headquarters. Keith was up on stage with the other Conservative candidates from the Ottawa area. Conservative leader Stephen Harper was there, too, and one of the first things Harper said was that if the Conservatives were elected, he'd hold a free vote on same-sex marriage.

I was more than just a little upset. Back in June 2005, the Liberal government had passed a same-sex marriage law by the narrowest of margins. The proposed law had passed second reading in the House of Commons on May 4. Had it not been for the Conservative MP Belinda Stronach crossing the floor to become a minister in Paul Martin's cabinet on May 17, the same-sex marriage bill would likely have died, because only two days after Stronach switched sides, the Martin government survived a confidence motion by only a single vote: 153-152. Stronach saved the government. The third reading of the same-sex marriage bill passed on June 28. So, Belinda Stronach should be the patron saint of same-sex marriage in Canada!

But now, the law was at risk again, thanks to the party I'd just joined. I noted my disappointment on my GayandRight blog and I sent Keith a private email letting him know my concerns. But when I spoke with Keith on the telephone, he insisted that Harper was just playing to his base and a free vote would amount to nothing anyway. When the issue came up later in the campaign debates, Harper said he supported "similar rights and benefits for all other equivalent relationships." What did that mean? How can you have similar rights and benefits for same-sex couples, but not have same-sex marriage? Were we arguing over a term? Would it be illegal for gay couples to refer to themselves as being married?

Fortunately, Harper said he would accept the result of a free vote, and also that he would not use the notwithstanding clause to upturn a Supreme Court finding in favour of same-sex marriage. This left me hoping that the Conservatives would win only a minority government, because then it would be doubtful that the former Liberal government's same-sex law would be thrown out.

With that at the back of my mind, I worked hard on Keith's campaign. I enjoyed myself. And I learned things.

One of the more amusing moments occurred at the offices of A-Channel, a local TV station, for a Breakfast TV debate. Before the show began, we said our hellos to the NDP's Paul Dewar and the Liberals' Richard Mahoney, and then the Green Party's David Chernushenko came up to us and asked Keith if he knew what the Israelis had just done. We didn't have a clue what he was talking about. Chernushenko told us that they were dumping nuclear waste in the Golan Heights. I gave Keith a look — the Israelis may be dumb, I thought, but they're not that dumb. Why was the Green Party candidate so excited by such weird rumours about Israel?

I learned later that David's father was Anton Chernushenko, a retired Canadian diplomat who was known for spending his retirement years writing letters to the news media complaining about the Christian right, the pro-Israel lobby, "overblown" concerns about the Chinese government's massacre of the Tiananmen Square protestors, American "meddling" in the Balkans, and "the charnel house of the EU."

I guess the apple doesn't fall far from the tree.

The other particularly fun moment, although it was a bit unsettling, was an Ottawa-Centre appearance with the other candidates on CTV's afternoon political show, *Power Play*, hosted by Mike Duffy. Keith and

I showed up early and were taken into the makeup room. Duffy was there getting worked on. At the time I didn't even know Duffy was a conservative, but he tipped us off that during the interview he'd be raising the "sponsorship scandal" that was plaguing the Liberals during the campaign. By prepping Keith like that, Duffy was doing us a favour we didn't ask for, leaving Mahoney at a distinctly unfair disadvantage.

Prime Minister Harper would go on to appoint Duffy to the Red Chamber in 2008. Duffy would go on to disgrace himself as an expense-fiddling Conservative senator, causing no end of scandal and misery to Harper personally and the Conservatives generally.

One of the most enlightening campaign sessions was a Jewish Community Centre event. The editors of the Ottawa Jewish Bulletin were bringing the Ottawa candidates of each political party to the community centre, separately. At the Conservative session, with Keith and his fellow Conservative candidates — John Baird, Pierre Poilievre and Royal Galipeau — Baird, the senior Conservative, took control of the meeting. I was floored by his knowledge.

Baird not only knew a lot about Israeli history and Israeli politics, but he also seemed to know all the major people in the Jewish community. He answered questions with detailed replies and made it all look easy. It was clear that the other Conservatives candidates would probably have been largely at a loss if Baird hadn't been there.

Even though I'd become an active Conservative Party campaigner, I continued to maintain a critical distance from some aspects of the party and its policies, and I found that the Conservatives didn't seem to mind. That was nice to know. During the campaign I continued to criticize the party on my GayandRight blog. One post I titled "The Problem with the Conservatives," which was mainly about the party's tax-cut pandering in its promise to lower the Goods and Services Tax. In another, I wrote that Harper should be ashamed of himself for attempting to outdo even Bloc Québécois leader Gilles Duceppe in weakening the federal government. In another, titled "Seven Issues the Conservatives Won't Touch," I took on the party for failing to address global warming, immigration, divorce settlement and child custody, multiculturalism and political correctness, bilingualism, cooperation with the Americans, and Aboriginal policy. I later added supply management. Nobody said a word. If I'd been told to shut up, I would have quit the campaign.

The reason these issues meant a lot to me was mainly because, if the Conservative Party was going to be afraid to deal with these issues openly and honestly, the issues would never be properly addressed. The Conservatives wouldn't touch child custody injustices, for instance — specifically the judicial practice of favouring mothers as caregivers over fathers, who tended to be allowed only the role of "walking wallets." Attempts to remedy the situation with measures that afforded both parents equivalent access to their children had gone nowhere. In the case of bilingualism, just about anybody in Ottawa could tell stories about the policy's often ridiculous effects on the civil service. Enormous amounts of money were being spent on ineffective language training, and too many positions required a bilingual rating anyway. Civil servants were getting promoted more on the basis of language ability than on the basis of merit — but to raise this problem publicly was to risk being accused of insensitivity or even bigotry.

It was a long campaign. Right before the finish of the campaign, we found out what a friend Canada had in Michael Moore. He'd returned to his pet subject of Canada with a message for Canadian voters: "Do you want to help George Bush by turning Canada into his latest conquest? Is that how you want millions down here to see you from now on? The next notch in the cowboy belt? C'mon, where's your Canadian pride? I mean, if you going to reduce Canada to a cheap download of Bush & Co., then at least don't surrender so easily. Can't you wait until he threatens to bomb Regina? Make him work for it, for Pete's sake."

I guess Canadians weren't listening. The Conservatives won 124 seats, enough to form a minority government. Stephen Harper was sworn in as Canada's 22nd prime minister on Feb. 6, 2006. Sadly, Keith Fountain lost, but we kept in touch. We became good friends.

With the election behind me, I decided to pick up on that idea that

the Bytowne Theatre people had put into my head when they turned
down *Michael Moore Hates America*, the documentary I'd wanted them
to show: Why don't you bring in your own films?

So that's exactly what I started doing.

Four

Iranium

It was Jan. 11, 2007, and Carol Usher, the manager of the Rainbow Cinema in Ottawa, was on the phone. She wanted to know if the documentary I had booked to show at her theatre, *Obsession: Radical Islam's War Against the West* had been rated by the Ontario Film Review Board. I didn't have the faintest idea. I didn't know that films had to go through the Board at all.

Usher told me the theatre could not show my film until it had a rating, so I called the Board in Toronto and was quickly told that all documentaries are exempt. They don't require any ratings. I called Usher back to tell her, but she said it really didn't matter because the Rainbow Cinema had cancelled the showing. It seems that a retired Professor of History at Carleton University had sent an email complaining that the film maligned Muslims. And that was enough reason to cancel.

What a way to start a film society!

It was after the Bytowne Cinema had refused to bring in *Michael Moore Hates America* in late 2004 that the seed of the idea was planted: I should start bringing in films myself.

I'd come across the Liberty Film Festival in Los Angeles, which was devoted to conservative and libertarian films. In November 2005, I had again contacted Bytowne asking them if they might show some of the films from the festival, but that time around I didn't even get a reply.

I'd noticed that *Obsession* had been awarded the Liberty Film Festival's Best Feature Film prize, and I decided that perhaps it was time to get serious about bringing in films myself. Besides, *Obsession* seemed even more timely and more important than *Michael Moore Hates America* had been at the time. I had no experience in showing films, or even in putting on any type of show or concert, but one of my friends from the Right Book Club, Tony Hahn, was very interested in helping out. We put together a small group and started having regular meetings over dinner at my house to discuss how to proceed.

The first thing we had to do was find a venue, and the Rainbow Cinema, in the St. Laurent Shopping Centre, seemed the perfect choice. They rented out the theatre for only $400, the theatre could seat more than three hundred people, and they could project a film from a DVD. When I met with Carol Usher I'd brought background information about *Obsession*; I figured she'd want to know what the film was about and I wanted to be completely open about our plan. We discussed how the cinema operated, and I agreed to rent the space for a Jan. 29, 2007, showing. I also paid half of the $400 rental fee up front. I issued a press release on Nov. 17, 2006, announcing the film showing.

So when Usher told me on the phone that she was backing out, I was shocked. It was a little more than two weeks before the film showing.

Usher said she'd received a complaint via email. She'd forwarded me the email and asked whether the Rainbow theatre company should be concerned ("I do not want to have the name of the Rainbow Cinemas tarnished in any way," she wrote). The complaint was from Siusaidh Campbell, PhD, retired professor of history at Carleton University: "Don't you find anti-Muslim stereotypes, which is to say misrepresentation and lies, are current enough without your offering the Ottawa public, "Obsession"? This is really unwise, and hurts the thousands of Capital Region Muslims, and friends of Muslims such as myself. Please add my name to those protested [sic] Rainbow's Cinema's further politicization of movie-going." There was nobody else protesting that I knew about. I'd emailed Usher to tell her that she had nothing to worry about, that this person could not have even seen the movie, since *Obsession's* producers make it clear in the documentary that most Muslims are peaceful, caring people. But, no matter. Within minutes of talking to Usher on the telephone she sent me another email: "I just received word from Head Office, and I am sorry to say we cannot play this movie for you."

I was stunned. One email from the public, and a fairly large corporation had given in. No discussion. No debate. They never even asked to watch the film to make up their own minds.

Obsession is a 75-minute film that traces the rise of radical Islam and its incitement of global jihad. The film discusses genocidal theocratic groups like Hezbollah, Hamas and Al-Qaida. *Obsession* is very clear that Islam had been hijacked by dangerous ideologues who want to destroy the shared values of the west. Interviewed in the film are Sir Martin Gilbert, a well-known historian; Alan Dershowitz, a prominent defender of Israel; Daniel Pipes, an expert on Islam and Islamism; Khaled Abu Toameh, a Muslim Israeli journalist; Robert Wistrich, the foremost expert on anti-Semitism; Itamar Marcus, the founder of Palestinian Media Watch; and many others. The film opens with a note that says "It's important to remember, most Muslims are peaceful and do not support terror. This is not a film about them. This is a film about a radical worldview and the threat it poses to us all, Muslim and non-Muslim alike."

With the screening advertised for Jan. 29, just over two weeks away, I had to hustle and find a new venue. I called around and found a room at the Ottawa Public Library that was fortunately available on that date. The only problem was that the room had no projection facilities and so I had to rent video and audio equipment. That sent my costs surging dramatically and I knew that my loss would be substantial. I sent out a press release on Jan. 12 announcing the cancellation by the Rainbow Cinema, and this got picked up by the Ottawa Sun, which ran a major story on Jan. 25: "An Obsession with protests: Theatre cancels showing of movie after lone complainant tags it anti-Muslim without having even seen the film." The Rainbow Cinema head office refused to answer any questions, but Susan (aka Siusaidh) Campbell did send an email to the Sun Newspaper. She told them that "as a friend of several people who 'look Arab' or 'look Muslim' I figured efforts to discourage the Rainbow were appropriate."

The article noted that a Google search for Susan Campbell turned up "a number of causes she has attached her name to, including petitions to free a U.S. soldier court-martialed for refusing to fight in the Gulf War, another to stop bookstore W.H. Smith from selling Playboy products…" Publicity from the Ottawa Sun helped immensely. The 170-seat room at the Ottawa Public Library was completely sold out. Barbara Crook, the associate director of Palestinian Media Watch, opened the evening with a few comments. The evening was a complete success. We were off to an auspicious start.

I should have sent chocolates to Susan Campbell to thank her for putting us on the map.

I now had a team of four other people to help us move forward: Tony Hahn from the Right Book Club days; James Cohen, a local musician; Michael Wallack, a student; and Randy Kroeker, who also served with me on the Ottawa Centre Conservative EDA. We started to meet regularly at my house over dinner, and barnstorm ideas on what we should do next. And that's how the Free Thinking Film Society was born.

Tony also was very helpful in writing a description of what we were all about, and he came up with this fine paragraph:

The Free Thinking Film Society was established in 2007 in Ottawa to provide an outlet for filmmakers and moviegoers alike who are looking for an alternative to the 'alternative'. In other words, we celebrate the efforts of risk-taking documentarians whose work espouses the values of limited, democratic government, free market economies, equality of opportunity rather than equality of result, and the dignity of the individual, all underscored by a healthy and patriotic respect for Western culture and traditions. Although there are a lot of courageous voices in the non-fiction film industry producing thoughtful pieces of art which reject cultural relativism, central economic planning and American culpability for all that ills the world, you wouldn't know it by looking at the listings for most art house cinemas. We're dedicated to changing that by bringing these exciting and challenging documentaries to Canada's capital.

For our next event, we decided to stay at the Ottawa Public Library and show the film *Mine Your Own Business*, a terrific documentary about the dark side of environmentalism. The film covers the Roşia Montană gold-mining project in Romania and shows how foreign environmentalists tried to convince the government to stop the project from moving forward. The local population, mired in poverty and unemployment, are anxious for the 600 jobs the project would bring.

The best parts of the documentary are the scenes with Mark Fenn, from the World Wildlife Fund, who tries his best to convince local villagers in Madagascar that they do not need a mine that was being proposed, and that they would be happier without it. Fenn then proudly shows off his $35,000 sailboat.

Because of my success with *Obsession*, I got cocky and did very little promotion. And, not surprisingly, only 30 people showed up. It was a huge financial loss and a wake-up call to do more marketing.

The next film we showed was *Indoctrinate-U*, a truly excellent film on "political correctness" on campus. The film was made by a young conservative filmmaker, Evan Coyne Maloney, who visited various campuses across the United States to talk to students, professors and administrators. Maloney attempts to get university administrators on camera to discuss anti-free speech policies, with very little success. He shows the trajectory of "free speech" movements on campus in the 1960s that ended up morphing into their opposite, in the form of left-wing and ideologically rigid faculties that suppressed debate and contrary ways of thinking.

Just before the film showing I was contacted by a professor at the University of Ottawa, Denis Rancourt, who was also showing documentaries on a regular basis, but with a left-wing perspective. He wanted to share perspectives on "free thinking" and I thought that perhaps we might collaborate on something in the future.

When I checked his website — Cinema Politica: Screening Truth

to Power — I could see that he was showing typical "alternative" post-
modern left-wing films. For instance, *The Power of Community: How
Cuba Survived Peak Oil* was a film about how Cuba "transitioned from
a high mechanized, industrial agricultural system to one using organic
methods of farming and, local urban gardens;" *The World Stopped
Watching*, a sympathetic look back at the Sandinistas in Nicaragua;
Salud a look at Cuba, a cash-strapped country with what the BBC calls
"one of the world's best health systems;" and *Live Nude Girls Unite* about
the first strippers union in the United States.

I called Rancourt. It was not a pleasant conversation. He said he
hated capitalism and went apoplectic when I told him I had enjoyed my
nine years working for Intel. To him, this could not have been possible.
Corporations gave orders, they told people how and what to think and
were soulless places where individuals just worked for profit. It seemed
inconceivable to him that anybody could enjoy life within a corporation.

I asked him if any of his students would like to attend *Indoctrinate-U*
and he said that he would send a few students to check it out. Two of
Rancourt's students did attend our showing, and they introduced
themselves after the film. They clearly did not like the documentary, but
I didn't have much time to talk to them. I had to organize the reception
after the film. I gave them my card and I asked them to email me their
impressions.

The next day I received an email from "M.P." who wrote that
"without any kind of ideological bias, I must say the movie *Indoctrinate-U*
was highly disappointing. One might, as your guest-speaker suggested
[Ottawa Citizen columnist John Robson] be against Michael Moore's
movies, I agree, but at least, as movies, I must highlight Moore's have
a minimum touch of cinematic quality. As a "Film Society", I hope the
future films to be featured are better directed and produced ones than
the one showed this evening. As for the content, the movie as well as your
guest-speaker had hollow arguments and very paradoxical rhetorics. I
hope, for your society's own sake (I don't share much of your opinions,
and I found much of the views expressed tonight as being reductive,

exclusive, and redundant), that you engage in more rigorous debates, without, of course, being less polemical. Moreover, it is strange that you victimize yourselves as it is evident, in general, that echoes of your views are found in great numbers in universities in Quebec, Canada, and, of course, the 'states.'"

Huh?

I entered his email text into Google translate but it was stumped too. I couldn't help myself and I sent him a reply asking if he had any specific comments about the film. He never answered.

I later found that Professor Denis Rancourt had caused quite a stir at the University of Ottawa in 2005 when he turned his entry-level Physics and Environment class into a course on activism and in 2008 when all 23 students, in his fourth-year courses, were awarded an A+ grade. Rancourt then taught a Science in Society class and brought in Malalai Joya, a discredited member of the Afghan Parliament, who opposed the NATO mission in that country. Rancourt had written in Canadian Dimension that Joya's talk was "a sharp blade cutting thru the thick web of US-Canada war propaganda: We have helped to install war lords and human rights abusers in a mock democratic process characterized by power relations and geo-political design. The Canadian army serves political aims and is contributing to making life worse for the people of Afghanistan than under the oppressive Taliban regime."

Really? Millions of girls were going to school in Afghanistan and yet life was supposedly worse than under the Taliban?

(The university administration ended up firing Rancourt, who promptly filed a $10 million lawsuit, arguing that his dismissal was related to his views on the Israel-Palestine conflict and that University of Ottawa President Alan Rock was "a point-man of the Israel lobby at the University of Ottawa." Unsurprisingly, Rancourt lost his case.)

As a new film society in Ottawa, it was hard getting press attention, but I was delighted when the weekly free event newspaper, Ottawa Xpress, showed some interest in reviewing our films. The first Ottawa Xpress review of a Free Thinking Films documentary was about *Che:*

Anatomy of a Myth, which presents Che Guevara not as a romantic hero, but as a murderous thug. Editor Cormac Rea gave it a fairly positive review and provided some needed exposure for us.

This wouldn't last. The gloves came off when we showed a double bill of *The Case for Israel*, a film based on Alan Dershowitz's book of the same name, and *The Monster Among Us*, a film about anti-Semitism in Europe. Rea found that the film on anti-Semitism was "an awful mess of shock and awe tactics and blatant fear mongering," but did not mention any specific scenes he found offensive. His advice was "to save your dime for an actual work of investigative journalism."

Fair enough. Any publicity is good publicity.

Our next film sent Cormac Rea into a complete rage. The film, *Media Malpractice: How Obama got elected and Palin was targeted*, shows how the news media treated Obama with kid gloves during the 2008 campaign, but went after Palin without mercy. The documentary presents hundreds of media clips showing a fawning press completely enamoured with Obama, and thus the media failed to properly vet Barack Obama's candidacy.

(I should point out that from the beginning I considered Sarah Palin unqualified to be vice president and that John McCain had made a huge mistake in her nomination. I wrote on my blog that my personal preference for president was Obama, and that was largely because of McCain's poor judgement in teaming up with Palin. That being said, I agreed with the premise of the film that Palin was treated horribly by the press.)

In his review, Rea started off by asserting that there was "a danger in drawing attention to films put on by Free Thinking," and that "at the end of the day, these amateur works of celluloid offer some of the most twisted, backwards arguments I've ever witnessed, built on heavily skewed logic that only people with angry-short-man syndrome could love." Wow. I've never heard of angry-short-man syndrome. How did Rea figure out that I am only 5'8"?

But, here's the kicker. "While [filmmaker John] Ziegler laments the 'death of journalism,' the roots of shock and awe television during the Bush years and the indefensible steps taken during his Oval Office tenure to limit the rights of the press are completely ignored in *Media Malpractice*. Obama's appeal — clearly expressed policies, soaring oratories, rights for all rhetoric — was literally an ideological ray of light after the pigs-will-fly hyperbole that had previously run rampant under the Republicans. It's no wonder biblical language was finally invoked by the media."

Gee, did I miss something? What steps did Bush take to limit the rights of the press?

Rea concluded that "if you're the type of person who likes to rehash yesterday's news faster than an infant's second plate of mashed potatoes, go see this flick. If not, appreciate that we live in a society where any nutbar can speak his opinion, however comical that may be."

Four months later, Mark Leiren-Young, a freelancer for Ottawa Xpress had a chance to interview Michael Moore regarding his new documentary, *Capitalism: A Love Story*. Leiren-Young was no ordinary reporter. He was the winner of the 2009 Stephen Leacock Medal for Humour for his best-selling memoir, *Never Shoot a Stampede Queen: A Rookie Reporter in the Cariboo*. But, Leiren-Young was in love — "So, when I found out I could interview Moore about his latest autopsy of the American Dream, *Capitalism: A Love Story*, after the film's North American premiere at the 2009 Toronto International Film Festival, I was practically giddy." He goes on: "When Moore walked by me in the hall of the Hotel Intercontinental wearing jeans, a T-shirt, a Commie-red Rutgers University ball cap and sneakers and said 'hi' before disappearing into a room to wait for his interviews, I was star-struck."

During the interview, Leiren-Young suggested to Moore that "in Canada there's nothing in capitalism a Grade 8 social studies teacher would get in trouble for teaching, but in the U.S. questioning the merits of their economic system will have people accusing him of treason. Moore agrees." To end his fawning article, Leiren-Young "thanked Moore for the 'za [pizza]. He apologized that it was cold. I wouldn't have cared if it was frozen."

Once I saw this article, I just couldn't resist emailing Cormac Rea and asking him why his newspaper wasn't as critical of Moore as he had been about Free Thinking Films. He replied that "that piece was done in a first person style by a writer who had the unique opportunity to have lunch with Moore at TIFF," and "additionally, the 'giddy' writer adeptly qualified his interest in Moore with one revealing sentence: "I think what he does — or at least tries to do — is important enough that I don't obsess over how he does it."

Over the next few years, we also regularly brought in speakers, and in November 2010 I organized the First Annual Free Thinking Film Festival. Among the events I presented were *Do As I Say*, a great film on liberal hypocrisy; *U.N. Me*, a critical look at the United Nations; a panel on Afghanistan that raised some money for the Afghan School Project in Kandahar; *The Soviet Story*, a film about the crimes of the Soviet Union; Crossing, a tearjerker of a film that the Wall Street Journal called the "Schindler's List for North Korea"; *Reclaiming Pride*, a film about how Queers Against Israeli Apartheid brought a message of hate to Toronto's gay pride march; *The Lives of Others*, a terrific film about the horrifying system of observation in the former East Germany; *Mr. Conservative,* an affectionate profile of American conservative Barry Goldwater; *For Neda*, a film about Neda Agha-Soltan, who was shot and killed on the streets of Tehran during the uprising in 2009; *Outside the Great Wall*, an examination of 12 Chinese intellectuals working for democracy in China; *Mugabe and the White African*, about one of the last white farmers in Zimbabwe; and *The Stoning of Soraya M*, which depicts a stoning in a small village in post-revolutionary Iran.

The centrepiece of that first film festival was a debate between Ezra Levant and Elizabeth May on the Alberta oil sands. I had been friendly with Ezra for a while and he was keen to debate anybody over his new book, *Ethical Oil*. I'd approached author and anti-oil activist Andrew Nikiforuk who had already debated Ezra in Alberta, but Andrew was busy that weekend, so I went with Green Party leader and well-known environmentalist Elizabeth May. I had the idea of asking Elizabeth when I noticed the Green Party's display at Confederation Park during the Gay Pride march that year. . .I'd left them my card. To my delight, before I knew it Elizabeth was scheduled to debate Ezra.

I knew this was going to be big. First step was to find an objective moderator, someone who would be acceptable to both sides. So, I reached out to my friend, well-known author and columnist Terry Glavin, who had previously been a panellist at one of our earlier events. Both sides were amenable to having Terry moderate, and so we were set.

We sold over 350 seats and the debate was amazing. Ezra made the case that Canadian oil is more "ethical" than oil from countries like Saudi Arabia. May made the case that we should get off oil entirely. The debate was friendly and had some terrific exchanges. There was no clear winner and partisans of both sides had their moments. The debate was also videotaped by CPAC and remained online on YouTube.

It was a crowning achievement for Free Thinking Films.

Our next event, scheduled for Tuesday, Jan. 18, 2011, was the film *Iranium*, by the same people who produced *Obsession* — our first film, the one that had frightened the Rainbow Theatre. *Iranium* is about the brutality of the Iranian regime and its long and covert quest for nuclear weapons. Along with the film showing, I'd decided to fly in Clare Lopez, an outspoken former operations officer with the CIA and an expert on jihad and counter-terrorism who appears in the documentary. Since the showing was slated for the middle of winter I'd expected a relatively small crowd. I figured it would be a minor event for the Society.

Little did I know what was about to happen.

Although I was unaware of it at the time, the trouble started on Thursday, Jan. 13, only five days before the event was scheduled, with a telephone call to the Federal Government's Library and Archives Canada from the Iranian embassy. The embassy wanted the film showing cancelled, and demanded a meeting between Kambiz Sheikh-Hassani, the Head of Iran's diplomatic mission, and Daniel Caron, Librarian and Archivist of Canada. After the Iranian embassy's involvement was revealed, the drama would go on to become a national and international story involving diplomatic tensions, protests, mysterious envelopes filled with white powder, and a huge debate about free speech. This was a much bigger deal than I'd had to cope with over the Rainbow Theatre's overreaction to Obsession.

The first sign that something was afoot came to my attention on the Monday following the embassy's Thursday call to the Library and Archives. I was driving to Loblaws supermarket and the liquor store to buy food and drink for the post-showing reception, and my phone rang. It was Marc Delorme, the Library and Archives' event coordinator. Delorme told me that there had been complaints about the film, and that the Library and Archives had no choice but to cancel the showing. Of course, they would help me find another venue to show the film, Delorme said.

Since I was in my car talking on a Bluetooth connection to my cellphone, I agreed to the help Delorme was offering, but I protested that it was going to be next to impossible. The film was to be shown the following night.

I realized that I had to get home as soon as possible, and almost right away I got another call from Delorme. He told me he'd determined that the Canadian Museum of Nature was available for a fee of $1,350. This was far pricier than the Library and Archives' fee (a mere $180), so I asked Delorme whether I'd be compensated for the difference. Delorme said I'd hear back from the Archives about that.

I then called Film Society board members Roy Eappen and Tamara Fulmes for advice. After a quick conversation, we agreed that we'd been put in an impossible situation, that it was far too late to change venues, and we had to insist on showing the film at the Library and Archives as planned. When Delorme called back a short while later to say the Library and Archives would pick up the fee at the Museum of Nature, I told him thanks, but no thanks — we were going to have to show the film at the Library and Archives. It was too late to change venues.

I then called the office of James Moore, the Federal Minister of National Heritage — the department responsible for Library and Archives Canada. I calmly explained my plight to a staff member (I'd also sent an email to Moore through the official Department website). Within a half hour, I got a call back from one of Moore's senior staffers. I described in detail what had transpired — or rather what I knew about what had transpired.

At about 6:30 that evening I got a call from the Library and Archives' Stuart Campbell ("Senior Director General of Business Integration and Strategies"), who told me the film showing was back on. That evening I sent out an email to Film Society supporters and our news media contact list about the "film that was almost banned." I'd written that "only a phone call from the office of the Minister of National Heritage, James Moore, led to its reinstatement."

The next morning I received an angry phone call from a senior official in James Moore's office (whose name I don't recall) who said I shouldn't have implied that it was pressure from the minister that changed the decision, because the Library and Archives is expected to operate at arm's length from the government. I responded that there were far more important issues at stake in the near-cancellation of the film showing than any minor indiscretion I may have committed in an email explaining what had occurred. For instance, what really happened? Who had complained? What was the real story?

The official's tone changed and he admitted that it was a complaint from the Iranian Embassy that was behind everything.

I was too busy that day with arrangements for the film showing to make a big deal with the news media about the Iranian embassy's interference, but just after 4 pm. I got a phone call from the Library and Archives' Stuart Campbell again. He said that there were protestors inside and outside the building, that they had called the RCMP, that the RCMP had decided that public safety could not be assured and that they had no choice but to cancel the film showing — again. The building had been shut down.

I called my friend James Cohen and told him what had just

happened. I hopped into my car, picked up James, and we drove to the Library and Archives on Wellington Street in downtown Ottawa near the Parliament buildings. We got there at about 4:50 pm. There were a few people milling around outside the building — mostly Library and Archives employees, but certainly no protestors. There was a sign on the door: "For reasons beyond our control, this building will be closed on Jan. 18, 2011, as of 4:45 pm. and for the entire evening. We will reopen for business tomorrow as usual."

Then the police showed up. Then the fire department showed up. My friend Roy Eappen was there. He'd been calling some of his media contacts, and so my cellphone started ringing. One call was from Alan Neal of the local CBC afternoon radio show. He wanted to go live on air, and I agreed. During the interview Neal seemed less interested in the bizarre circumstances surrounding the event's cancellation than in what my views were about the ministerial propriety of interventions from James Moore's office — which may or may not have resulted in the Library and Archives' reversal of its initial decision to cancel the event. Because I'd already had my knuckles rapped for implying that Moore's office had earlier intervened successfully on the event's behalf, I tried to avoid the subject. It was an awkward conversation, to say the least.

It was a very cold night and a bunch of us decided to reconvene at my house. My partner Andrew went off to buy Chinese food. I had no idea that as crazy as things were at that moment, my world was about to explode. There were about ten of us at my place and while we were eating dinner, I got a phone call from an Ottawa Citizen reporter insisting that she should come over immediately to interview me. I agreed. My landline and cellphone were ringing nonstop. I barely had time to eat. The emails were also coming in thick and heavy.

The following morning, the news media were filled with stories about Iranian attempts to shut down the showing of a film at a government building in Canada's capital city. Something I hadn't known that night on Wellington Street was that two "suspicious" envelopes had been hand-delivered that day to the Library and Archives (they were later examined by a Hazmat team and found to be harmless) by a man who had hurried away, and there had been threats of violence phoned in as well. Radio-Canada (French language CBC) came over to interview me for a television broadcast and Global TV arrived just as they left. Then I had to hurry over to Wellington Street for a CTV interview in front of the Library and Archives building. While I was making my way over, my phone was ringing nonstop. During calls, the call-waiting signal kept clicking. My voicemail kept filling up. It was a zoo. I ended up missing calls from Fox News in the United States, but I did manage to get back to a news outfit in Russia.

That morning, I'd received a telephone call from National Heritage Minister James Moore to ensure me that *Iranium* would be shown at the Library and Archives. They would be in touch to arrange it. In addition, the Canadian government sent a diplomatic note to Iran that stated "Canada is a free country and freedom of expression is a core value that won't be compromised."

Every major media organization (newspapers, TV, radio) in Canada covered the *Iranium* kerfuffle. The coverage was almost universally sympathetic to the free speech angle and to the importance of showing *Iranium* at the LAC in Ottawa and not at some other venue. The film itself was garnering a huge public relations windfall: the producers noted that "in the first 24 hours following the cancellation, *Iranium* was mentioned in 574 blog posts" on top of all the articles in major newspapers.

I'd suggested to Moore that he give a talk at the event when the film was eventually shown. He agreed and when the film was shown at the Library and Archives on Feb. 6, Moore gave a speech that earned him several standing ovations. The event was sold out and we had to turn 60 people away. As you might guess, there was a lot of sympathetic press coverage that day, too.

As documentaries go, there's nothing notably controversial about Iranium. The 70-minute film opens with the Islamic Revolution in 1979 and subjects the sadistic ideology of Ayatollah Khomeini to close scrutiny, exposing his regime's hateful violence and oppression of the

Iranian people. The documentary tracks the theocracy's use of terror, beginning with the 1979 seizure of the American Embassy in Tehran and the hostage drama there that carried on for 444 days. Narrated by Shohreh Aghdashloo, the Tehran-born, Oscar-nominated actor who left the country during the Khomeinist revolution, Iranium also documents the regime's deployment of terrorist proxies around the globe. The film relies heavily on interviews with some of the regime's most outspoken American critics, including former CIA director James Woolsey; Foundation for Defense of Democracies founder Clifford May; and the historian Bernard Lewis, one of the foremost experts on the Middle East.

Iranium is clearly not a film the Iranian regime would be happy about, but as I was to learn later from material I gathered via an Access to Information request, Library and Archives officials deliberately misrepresented the extent of their dealings with the Iranian embassy at the time. Further, the decisions the Library and Archives brass was making about *Iranium* appear to have been motivated at least in part from a sense of obligation to the embassy, owing to a previous encounter with embassy officials.

The most disturbing revelation in the documents I obtained was that Library and Archives officials went out of their way to hide what was really going on during those hectic days in January 2011, and took pains to mislead the news media.

I'd been told explicitly, the day before the film was to be shown, that Library and Archives management had decided to cancel the showing — Delorme went as far to find the film an alternative venue (at the Museum of Nature) and agreed to cover the difference in fees. But that same morning, Library and Archives management issued a kind of party-line instruction to senior staff, in the form of a "Q&A," dealing with how to explain what was going on. One question was: "The Free Thinking Film Society alleges that LAC wanted to cancel this event. Is this true?" The party-line answer: "LAC [Library and Archives Canada] did receive a formal request from the Embassy of Iran to cancel this event. Further to this request, LAC assessed the risks associated with holding this event and decided that nothing justified its cancellation."

That was an outright falsehood. So was this: "While this decision was being made, LAC did contact the Free Thinking Film Society to alert them of the situation." In fact, I was contacted not to be "alerted" to a complaint, but to be told that the decision had been made and the event had been cancelled. Internal emails between Library and Archives officials also confirm the fact of the officials' decision to cancel.

The lie was reiterated in a media call "routing slip" referring to an inquiry from a Sun Media reporter. The Library and Archives' official account of its statement to the reporter, by email, was that indeed the Iranian embassy had sent a letter setting out is objections to the film showing and had also requested that the event be cancelled. "The objections of the Embassy were considered, however a decision was made to allow the Society to screen the film on the appointed date."

That was completely untrue. The decision was to cancel the event, and the Library and Archives' misrepresentations were successful in misleading the news media. The Ottawa Citizen, for instance, reported that "the Iranian Embassy had made a formal complaint requesting the cancellation. However, she [Pauline Portelance, spokesperson for LAC] denied that the cancellation had anything to do with the formal complaint." In a CBC report: "LAC spokesperson Pauline Portelance said the Embassy asked the Library not to show the film on the weekend, but that request was denied. Portelance said the screening was only cancelled once, on Tuesday, following a 'series of threats.'" This was also untrue — the screening had been cancelled twice. The CBC also accepted the untrue Library and Archives' "media line" as fact, reporting that Library and Archives managers "never requested that screening organizers find another venue."

Just as dishonest were the Library and Archives; public statements explaining management's last-minute decision to cancel the Jan. 18 showing owing to security concerns. Senior staff were instructed to explain the situation this way: "LAC did receive a formal request from the Embassy of Iran to cancel this event. However, it is only when

LAC received several threats of public protests that it deemed the
risk associated with this event too high and decided to close down
395 Wellington." This was worse than "spin." Library and Archives
officials were hiding the fact of their initial cancellation, in response to
the Iranian embassy's complaint, behind the subsequent alarm about
security concerns.

The Iranian embassy's explicit request that the film showing be
cancelled is contained in an inarticulate letter embassy officials wrote
to Library and Archives management Jan. 13, several days before the
scheduled event: "Library and Archives Canada as a valuable and
important resource is less likely to be used facilitating activities whose
intention is solely spreading hatred and sending revulsion messages to
the viewers and also embarking on fund raising for their inappropriate
activities by way of selling tickets," embassy officials complained. "The
Embassy, considering the nature of this gathering, strongly objects
permitting this program to be carried and hopes the esteemed office
of the Librarian and Archivist of Canada takes the needed measures of
prohibiting this activity to be conducted."

The internal documents I obtained in my Access to Information
request clearly show that, contrary to its statements to the news media,
Library and Archives brass had caved in to embassy. On Monday, Jan.
17, at 10:46 am., Laura Veitch, project officer in the Business Integration
Office, wrote this email to staff: "Mr. Caron [Librarian and Archivist of
Canada Daniel Caron] was internally advised to cancel the event." Ten
minutes later, Fabien Lengellé, Director General of the Communications
Bureau, sent this email to Mireille Miniggio, Director of Partnerships
and Public Programming: "M. Caron a décidé d'annuler l'événement
[Mr. Caron has decided to cancel the event]." In a subsequent internal
email, Lengellé noted that Iranian embassy had been advised of the
decision to cancel, and were quite pleased: "Ils sont très heureux de cette
décision [They were very happy with our decision]."

Two months later, an internal media analysis conducted by
the Library and Archives management set out quite clearly that

management's decision was to cancel the event, and the decision was in direct response to the embassy's complaint letter. The analysis states, in its opening paragraphs: "On Monday, January 17th, LAC who had allowed the Free Thinking Film Society to show it there, *cancelled the film on behalf of this request* [emphasis added]."

As for why it was that the Library and Archives Canada would adopt such an accommodating posture towards a bellicose foreign government (the following year, the federal government closed the Iranian embassy in Ottawa, expelled Iranian diplomats from Canada and shuttered Canada's embassy in Tehran), and cover it up to boot, an earlier incident might explain things.

In July 2010, responding to pressure from Iranian diaspora groups, the Library and Archives cancelled an official embassy event that was to be held that October at the Wellington Street headquarters. Billed as "A Window to the Sun's Land," it was to be an evening highlighting Iranian architecture, "handicrafts" and a documentary film on Iranian culture, with a lecture and a reception. An internal Library and Archives memo I obtained in my Access to Information request, written by Laura Veitch in the Business Integration Office, explained that the decision to cancel Iranium was, partly, "due to this previous decision."

As for the angry call I got from James Moore's office after I'd circulated a statement thanking the minister for intervening to overturn the decision to cancel the Iranium showing (in apparent contravention of the government's "arms-length" policy), it turns out that I'd got it right from the beginning. An internal email written by Fabian Lengellé, the Library and Archives' head of communications, notes quite explicitly "the minister's office overturned our decision." Further, the Library and Archives management chose to deliberately mislead the public about that, too. In another email, Lengellé states that "to the public at large, we will not even address this issue," and Stuart Campbell, Veitch's boss and the official who called me that the film showing was back on, confirmed the strategy. "Just to be clear should it be raised . . . the decision was made by LAC officials," Campbell wrote, and in dealing with the news media, "lines should state that the decision was made by officials."

The Library and Archives appears to have been swamped with complaints about the film showing's cancellation — its records show that by 2:43 pm. on Jan. 19, 60 calls about the incident had been logged by its call centre — and I'd also received hundreds of emails. Many came from Iranian émigrés. One Iranian-Canadian, a lawyer and pro-democracy activist, complained that the Iranian regime's embassy seemed to have a great deal of influence in Canada, adding: "I have been fighting against the Islamic Regime for close to 10 years, and I wanted to share my disgust with what has happened here." Another Iranian-Canadian wrote: "I thought we'd left this behind when we left Iran and now they have influence here."

There were exceptions to the sympathetic news coverage, though.

The Ottawa Citizen ran a front page story that also ran across Canada in other Postmedia newspapers highlighting worries about the incident worsening the "already-sour" relations between Iran and Canada. Under the headline "Documentary Spat Worsens Canada-Iran Relations," the article quoted Houchang Hassan-Yari, head of the department of politics and economics at the Royal Military College in Kingston: "It gives more ammunition to those in Iran who say, 'We told you the Canadians were this and that'....in other words, discrediting the whole notion of the human rights question raised by the Canadian government (before the United Nations and elsewhere)."

The professional foreign affairs clique also had to get into the action. In an Ottawa Citizen opinion essay, John Mundy, former Ambassador to Iran, wrote that Iranium was insufficiently sympathetic to the Iranian regime in failing to deal critically with the CIA involvement in the coup of the 1950s, western indifference to Iraq's use of weapons of mass destruction in its war with Iran, and the significance of attempts by Iran's "reformist" president Mohammad Khatami to reach out to the United States following 9/11. To the Ottawa Citizen's arts reporter Jamie Portman, the bigger worry was that a Heritage Minister had "violated the arms-length relationship that exists between independent federal cultural agencies and politicians." To Portman, this threatened to be a tipping point, a harbinger of the new Conservative governments plan to return to the bad old days of "ministerial control over cultural agencies."

While the Film Society was gathering supporters, I was also attracting quite a few critics.

Among my detractors was Yahya Abdul Rahman, a local Muslim convert who speculated that the incident was a "false flag" operation, and that some "political entity" had orchestrated everything to "make Iran look bad." In a blog post, Rahman wrote: "Did Litwin and his Israel Lobby friends want just a little too much to create the impression there was an Iranian threat — even here in Ottawa?" He went on: "Litwin is so anti-Islam, pro-war and foremostly pro-Israel he could pass muster for a straight Christian Zionist. And he is nothing if not a rabid, but somewhat clumsy political hound." (I ended up having to block Rahman from my email inbox after he'd refused to stop flooding me with anti-Israel material.) Then there was the popular Liberal Party blogger Michael J. Murphy ("BigCityLib") who proposed an alternative conspiracy theory — the standoff with the embassy was just a public-relations stunt. "I'm not accusing anyone, I'd just point out that stunts are not unheard of. Watch as this story evolves." Murphy carried on in this way for a while. I eventually managed to get Murphy to apologize. John Baglow, a retired union official in Ottawa whose blog "Dr. Dawg" was particularly popular among ultra-hysterical Canadian "left-wingers," was upset with how things had turned out. "Fred Litwin is happy as a pig in the proverbial cesspool," Baglow wrote. "Fred Litwin couldn't have counted on a better result if he'd planned the whole thing himself."

But as free speech victories go, the *Iranium* controversy was a mixed blessing.

Planning for the eventual Feb. 6 showing was a nightmare. There were several security meetings I had to attend, involving the Ottawa Police and several government departments. RCMP Inspector Bruce Kirkpatrick of the Protective Policing Service was brought in because

James Moore, a cabinet minister, was scheduled to talk. Robert Metalie, the RCMP Technical Security Officer was brought in. A variety of new security procedures were implemented coat-checks were to be mandatory, and all purses and backpacks had to be checked by the police prior to entry. The day of the event, RCMP sniffer dogs were brought in to ensure no one was hiding anything. The Library and Archives' Reading and Consultation rooms were closed all day. There were 17 security guards on hand. The Library and Archives spent a total of $15,000 on extra security that day, I was told.

In Tehran, Iran's Foreign Affairs ministry issued a statement describing the events in Ottawa as "a clear example of Canada's Iran phobia policy that Ottawa has chosen." The following month, when *Iranium* was shown at York University in Toronto, about 60 students organized by the pro-regime Iranian Students Association showed up to protest the film showing at the Computer Science and Engineering Centre. The film had been moved to the Centre because of what Toronto police called an "unspecified threat" when the film was originally booked for another building, Vari Hall. When the film was eventually shown, 11 Toronto police officers and York University security were on hand.

Another effect of the *Iranium* controversy was that it caused the Library and Archives to decide that it was just too much trouble to allow its auditorium to continue as an important and cost-effective venue in Ottawa's cultural scene.

The year Iranium was shown, the auditorium was booked for 288 days by the Canadian Film Institute, the EU Film Institute, the Ontario Genealogy Society, the British Isles History Society and other such groups. There were festivals such as Black History Month, Asian Heritage Month, the Ottawa Jazz Festival and the Ottawa Children's Festival. The documents I obtained by my Access to Information request showed that Iranium was seen as a last straw, and that providing space to non-governmental organizations was too much of a hassle. The way Assistant Deputy Minister Cecilia Muir put it was that "we definitely need to get out of this business."

The Library and Archives handed management of the auditorium to Public Works Canada, which began jacking up prices and fees, discouraging public use of the venue. From a cost of almost nothing, the price of renting the auditorium for an evening had skyrocketed by 2015 to $1,920. The auditorium is quiet most nights of the week. An important cultural space has been lost.

Hurrah to the Khomeinists.

Five

Stephen Harper's Holy War on Homos

It was September 2010 and my friend Roy Eappen, a fellow conspirator in the Free Thinking Film Society, wanted to know if Andrew and I wanted to fly down to New York City to attend Homocon, a fundraising party by a new gay conservative group, GOProud. The affair required a donation of $500, and the special guest was going to be the raging right-wing author-celebrity Ann Coulter. I was not then (and am not now) what you would call a fan of Ann Coulter, for any number of reasons, not least because in 2009 she'd signed something called the Manhattan Declaration, drafted by Watergate-era ne'er-do-well Chuck Colson, who'd gone on to become some kind of Christian evangelical. The declaration referred to homosexual conduct as "immoral" and claimed that the common good of civil society is "damaged" when jurisdictions recognize same-sex marriages.

But, the more I thought about it, the more I thought the spectacle of Coulter at Homocon might be something worth taking in. Was Ann changing, or were we in for a train wreck? Either way, it would be entertaining, and it was in New York City, so why not?

The party was to be held at billionaire Peter Thiel's swank new apartment right across from Union Square (Thiel was co-founder of PayPal and an early investor in Facebook). It was going to start at 6:30 pm. and end at 8:00 pm. so we arrived early to ensure we didn't miss a minute.

While we were waiting in the lobby for the green light to go upstairs, we were entertained by lovely go-go boys wearing very tight "freedom is fabulous" t-shirts. At about 6:25 p.m., we were allowed into the elevator and 11 of us piled in. The door closed and the elevator went up a few inches, lurched and went back down about three feet. The door wouldn't open and the buttons weren't working.

We were stuck in an elevator in midtown Manhattan. We were packed in like sardines, yelling for help. Somebody on the other side of the door yelled back that they'd call the manufacturer of the elevator. We yelled again: no, call the fire department!

The firefighters got there in amazingly quick time, probably 20 minutes, and they got the door open almost right away. We all decided to walk up the four floors rather than risk the elevator again, and by the time we walked into Thiel's place, which took up the whole floor of the building and must have cost him millions, the party was going strong. Nobody knew about our ordeal in the elevator and our arrival was completely ignored. I bought a drink and started mingling. Coulter was schmoozing around the room, and soon enough she'd set up behind a corner table with her notes, and her "show" got under way. Coulter's routine was funny enough, although each joke was printed on separate pieces of paper. Gee, I thought, most comedians memorized their material, no?

I decided to move to the food table. The party was going to be over quickly, and I figured it was a good idea to get to the food before the crowds moved in. So Andrew and I sat in the back of the room eating while everybody else was watching Coulter, and as soon as her monologue was done and the question-and-answer session began, a big argument broke out over same-sex marriage. It was boring and predictable. Coulter argued that procreation was central to the institution of marriage, and that civil rights didn't enter into the gay marriage debate. Everybody else argued that gay marriage was a civil rights issue. It descended into a bit of a shouting match. I just kept eating.

Coulter's presence at the GOProud fundraiser ended up getting lots of press, and of course there were some furious reactions from the right wing. Joseph Farrah, editor-in-chief of the conservative website World

Net Daily, fired Coulter from her gig as keynote speaker at his upcoming "Taking Back America" national conference. He slammed Coulter for associating with a group that that was fighting for same-sex marriage and openly gay people in the military and for the idea that "sodomy is just an alternate lifestyle." Coulter answered Farrah that she often spoke to groups she didn't fully agree with.

Coulter's appearance at GOProud might seem like a trivial event, but it was a milestone in a huge debate that was beginning to open up among American conservatives, and particularly within the Republican Party. It wasn't that conservatives had just begun having arguments amongst themselves about homosexuality. GOProud was actually the second gay conservative group in the United States, the first being the Log Cabin Republicans, which had been founded back in the 1970s. The Log Cabin Republicans' first target was the Briggs Initiative in California, in 1977, which was a referendum on banning gays and lesbians from working in the public schools and authorizing the firing of teachers who even supported homosexuality. Interestingly, the conservative Republican hero Ronald Reagan, who was the governor of California at the time, opposed the referendum initiative. The measure lost by more than a million votes — 58 per cent opposed and 42 per cent in favour — and the turnout was really high: more than 70 per cent.

So, there had been splits among conservatives about homosexuality for quite a while, and it shouldn't be surprising that it was an uphill fight for gay rights in the Republican Party. American Conservatives see themselves as standard-bearers for a Judeo-Christian tradition that, let's face it, involves thousands of years of anti-homosexual teachings. It took the Stonewall riots in New York City in 1969 just to begin the process of getting liberals to embrace the gay community.

The story in Canada isn't all that different.

Homosexuality was decriminalized in Canada only in 1969 by a vote of 149-55 in the House of Commons; 12 Progressive Conservatives supported the motion and 43, including the former prime minister, John Diefenbaker, voted against. That omnibus bill also legalized contraception and therapeutic abortion. It's useful to recall some of the crazy things Canadian Conservatives were saying about homosexuality not that long ago. During the debate, Walter Carter (PC-St. John's West, Newfoundland) called homosexuality "a psychological aberration" that would cause society to break down if it got out of hand, and if "universally practiced," the human race would soon become extinct. Roch LaSalle (PC-Joliette, Quebec) said homosexuals were "probably sick people," and so should be confined in specially built hospitals to be subjected to treatment by specialists who would cure people of their "completely abnormal" illness. Walter Dinsdale (PC-Brandon–Souris, Manitoba) went so far as to accuse homosexuals of preying on children and called homosexuality "something that spreads like the plague, for there is no more destructive drive than the sexual impulse running wild." He then quoted Dante: "The hottest places in Hell are reserved for those who in a period of moral crisis maintained their neutrality."

The road from decriminalization to same-sex marriage in Canada took only 36 years, but the road to 2005 was paved largely by the courts, despite what the Liberal Party of Canada would now have you believe. In 1995, the Supreme Court of Canada ruled that the Charter of Rights and Freedoms should be interpreted to prohibit discrimination on the basis of sexual orientation, and then on May 19, 1999, the judges ruled that gays and lesbians should have the same rights as common-law couples with regard to pensions, taxes and other benefits.

Right after that ruling, on June 23, 1999, the House of Commons passed a Reform Party (then the Official Opposition) motion declaring that marriage was "the union of one man and one woman to the exclusion of all others." This motion won the support of the governing Liberals (including Prime Minister Jean Chretien and Finance Minister Paul Martin) by a vote of 216-55, with the New Democrats and the separatist Bloc Québécois voting against.

The following year, to comply with the Supreme Court ruling, the Liberal government passed Bill C-23 to extend benefits to common law same-sex marriages but which also included the traditional definition of marriage. In 2002-03, provincial court decisions in British Columbia, Quebec and Ontario held that the exclusion of gays and lesbians from the definition of marriage was contrary to the equality clause of the Canadian Charter of Rights and Freedoms. It was only from then that the federal Liberal Party supported same-sex marriage.

During House of Commons debates in response to the provincial court rulings in 2003, Elsie Wayne, a well-known Progressive Conservative MP from Atlantic Canada, said gay Canadians who wanted the right to marry should "shut up." But by this time, gay conservatives were becoming more outspoken within the party and James Murphy, president of Ottawa Vanier PC Youth, wrote a letter to the editor of a gay newspaper saying that Wayne's comments were "a disgrace."

Conservatives were starting to come onboard. But, in what might come as a shock to most people, the fight for same-sex marriage was vigorously opposed by a significant faction of the gay activist community.

One just has to read gay newspapers of the time to get a feel for the debilitating influence of what has been called the "post-modern left" on gay-identity politics — an influence that has the effect of encouraging indifference to emancipation, at best. Sometimes the result is an outright hostility to activism that would advance the cause of gay equality: better to be among the oppressed and the marginalized than to be among the emancipated.

Andrew Sullivan, in his book Virtually Normal, attributes this influence to an activist camp he refers to as the "liberationists," because of their assertions that homosexuality is just a "construct of human thought, not an inherent or natural state of being," and thus, there are no homosexuals — just the political choice to engage in homosexual acts. On this, the liberationists agree with the religious right, but their "prescription" is different. They desire to be "free of all social constructs," and thus age of consent, polygamy and marriage laws are all seen as an attack on, or an affront to, sexual freedom. But that's just where it starts.

The hero of the "liberationists," was Michel Foucault, the French philosopher who provided the intellectual underpinnings of the postmodernist movement. Foucault's claim is that that by creating the homosexual identity, "the modern West had simply replaced old chains with new ones." To Foucault, "the history of sexuality in the West is not a history from repression to liberation, but the exchange of one kind of power relations for another." Thus, gay identity is just "another prison," but to fix that, the family must be smashed and the "established heterosexual order" must be subverted, and in the meantime, the gay identity prison was where "liberationists" were content to remain.

What the task of subverting the heterosexual order implies for the "liberationists," Sullivan writes, is the necessity to "concentrate… on those instruments of power which require no broader conversation, no process of dialogue, no moment of compromise, no act of engagement." Sullivan concludes that liberationist politics is "almost always authoritarian. . . a strange confluence of political abdication and psychological violence."

Unfortunately, this camp has wielded an inordinate influence in Canada's gay community, and particularly in Canada's gay press.

The Body Politic, one of Canada's first major gay newspapers, was obsessed with polyamory, polygamy and intergenerational sex. In its first issue, an illustration depicts a man on the shoulders of the statue of King Edward VII at Queen's Park, site of the provincial legislature, in Toronto with the title "smash heterosexual imperialism." In August of 1972, the Body Politic published an article by Gerald Hannon, one of the newspaper's founding editors, under the headline "Of Men and Little Boys." In the article, Hannon — a veteran part-time sex trade worker and journalism professor at Ryerson University — argues that "loving a child and expressing it sexually is revolutionary activity. The activists of tomorrow are more than likely in someone's arms today." In late 1977, a Body Politic article titled "Men loving boys loving Men," which included a story about a man having sex with a 7-year-old, resulted in obscenity charges. The Body Politic was acquitted, and gained a status as a free-speech icon.

After The Body Politic closed in 1986 when its circulation dropped to just 7,000, its publisher, Pink Triangle Press (PTP) launched a new publication in Toronto called Xtra, which had begun as a supplement in The Body Politic in 1984. In 1993, PTP spun off two more tabloids, Xtra West in Vancouver and Capital Xtra in Ottawa.

In Capital Xtra's inaugural issue, editor Brandon Matheson stated that "with each issue, there are supporting and opposing views that must be given fair and equal treatment in a true journalistic style — accurate and objective," and that Capital Xtra will "respect, reflect, and report on the differences within our community…and celebrate them."

A fine statement, but as the evidence was to show, completely untrue. The Xtra newspapers would go on to become a repository for the worst kind of "queer politics": articles criticizing same-sex marriage because marriage itself was heterosexist, incomprehensible "queer theory" opinion pieces, a paranoid view of Canada and its culture, a "Chomskyite" view of international relations, and, predictably, an acute case of Harper Derangement Syndrome.

Just after 9/11, the well-known American gay-rights activist Rex Wockner described the Xtra newspapers in flattering terms as being motivated by "a kind of background disdain for capitalism as a religion — even as the publishers became decent capitalists so the papers could thrive." In the article, which appeared in Capital Xtra, Wockner said its publisher, PTP, "always has and continues to defend, if not promote, that which some people consider to be radical sex — promiscuity, intergenerational sex, public nudity, cruising, T-room sex [I had no idea what this was so I've had to look it up — it's homosexual sex in public toilets], open relationships, three-way (or more) relationships, fisting and pretty much anything else sexually edgy you can think of." Wockner added that PTP and its newspapers were also motivated by a "lack of love for the recently humbled USA. PTP papers are on a mission to change the world, not merely report on it."

Right from the start, the Xtra newspapers were so hostile to same-sex marriage that articles in Xtra West were used in B.C. court cases by anti-gay coalitions. This put the Xtra newspapers in a kind of alliance with the likes of the anti-feminist, anti-gay, REAL Women organization.

In British Columbia, Xtra West had run an article expressing the hope that a 2001 court challenge aimed at opening up same-sex marriage rights would fail, because gay marriage was bad for gay culture and gay liberation. It's no wonder, as I would later learn, that groups like REAL Women would scour the Xtra newspapers with care. I ended up coming across more than 30 REAL Women newsletters quoting articles from the Xtra newspapers to support their spurious claims that gay people oppose same-sex marriage, that gay people want to destroy the family, and that gay people are pedophiles who encourage intergenerational sex.

The disconnect between the PTP-Xtra establishment and mainstream gay opinion was especially obvious in an M. Anne Vespry Capital Xtra column in July 2005. She was angry about the gay community's embrace of marriage: "Is this all there is to a social revolution? Is this what I signed up for? I believed we could obtain equal rights — and sufficient day-to-day acceptance to avoid being beaten up — without changing ourselves. 'They' were supposed to accept our differences, not adopt or co-opt them. We were out to change the world — and we did — but I forgot to calculate the impact of the new world on queerdom. . .If we are the same as straights — except for the small matter of whom we choose to boink or marry — then remind me, please, what exactly we're so proud of."

There were times when Vespry's columns on the subject strayed into conspiracy theory. In November 2005, she asked: "Can the monogamously and matrimonially-focused activism of the 00s be partially attributed to AIDS having killed proportionately more of the most sex-positive members of our communities? An interesting question." In July that year, freelance writer Pat Croteau lamented the victories on the same-sex marriage front. "Around me people are cheering this historic occasion, but I find it hard to join in wholeheartedly. I am very concerned about the harm done to our community by this very conservative view of families."

In September 2006, after same-sex marriage had passed through

Parliament, Capital Xtra published a full-page feature headlined "Privatizing our Sex Lives: Same-sex marriage is just not enough, thank you." Its author, Toronto writer and academic Marusya Boclurkiw, wrote: "Marx and Engels were decidedly gloomy on the topic of marriage. According to them, marriage is a property relation, with its roots in slavery." Further, "same-sex marriage plays into the hands of a government hell-bent on privatizing everything from pension plans to healthcare." Boclurkiw was nostalgic for the good old days before marriage equality, when she "grooved to lesbianism's outlaw identity, its disdain of marriage, its freedom, and its abundant sex. . . I was living that utopian Marxist dream. I was nobody's property. Wedding dresses? Bridal veils? These were the last things I'd see at Dyke March or a Pride Parade." In a similar vein, PTP founder Charles Dobie lamented the state of the gay community in a December 2006 essay. "Gay people are becoming very complacent nowadays. Now, we can even get married. No one talks about different forms of sexuality or living arrangements, like communal marriages."

The influence of post-modernism, and the paradox of its desire for identity with the oppressed and the "other" that sometimes goes so far as to prefer the glamour of oppression over progressive emancipation, was on full display in the case of Capital Xtra columnist Ariel Troster.

While running a blog called Dykes Against Harper, Troster began to appear regularly in Capital Xtra in 2006, and would go on to leave her position as a board member of the gay rights group Egale (Equality for Gays and Lesbians Everywhere) on the grounds that Egale had become too mainstream. Troster was so concerned with maintaining gay identity in the category of the subaltern (a postmodernist classification of groups marginalized by capitalist and imperialist "hegemony") that she objected to campaigns against homophobia. Even the foundational gay movement position that "sexual orientation is not a choice" was enough to set her off. It bothered her almost as much as it annoyed old-school social conservatives.

Anti-homophobia activism "denies the entire thrust of the gay liberation movement," Troster wrote. Objecting to an anti-homophobia advertising campaign in 2007, Troster complained that the campaign undermined gay culture and its ideas, "which dared to suggest that queer people have something better to offer the world, a unique vision of sex, love and relationships, gleefully removed from hetero-normative values and the missionary position." To Troster, the notion that homosexuality was a normal state of being, rather than a conscious lifestyle choice, was "dangerous," because it could lead to "the same kind of gender and sexual essentialism that continues to oppress queer and trans people today."

Gareth Kirkby, the managing editor of Capital Xtra, was vehemently opposed to same-sex marriage, and considered the campaign for marriage rights a "tragic" diversion. In October 2007, Kirkby called marriage a heterosexual institution "designed by the church, endorsed by the state, with the intention of controlling the sexuality of women, and by extension, their husbands."

This same postmodernist stridency dominated the Xtra newspapers' coverage of a House of Commons effort, which enjoyed the support of all the parties, to raise the age of sexual consent in Canada from 14 to 16. The initiative, adopted in law in 2008, came in response to the 2005 case of Dale Eric Beckham, a 31-year-old from Texas (where the age of consent is 17) who had travelled to Ottawa to have sex with a 14-year-old boy. Police in Texas had found a huge cache of child pornography on his home computer, and in Ottawa the Conservative government expressed concern that predators from abroad could take advantage of Canada's relatively low age of consent in order to exploit Canadian children. Paul Gallant, managing editor of Toronto's Xtra, dismissed the initiative as a the fulfilment of Justice Minister Vic Toews' longtime fantasy to "criminalize sexually active youth."

The Xtra newspapers' editorial line tended to the position that the age of consent should be left at 14, lowered or eliminated entirely. Their attitude had changed little from days of The Body Politic and its "Men loving boys loving Men" article defending "intergenerational" sex, to the point of celebrating a man having sex with a 7-year-old boy.

In March 2006, Capital Xtra dedicated a large part of one issue to "teen sex rights" that featured a chart showing the age of consent around the world, but it showed only the age of heterosexual consent in various countries. I wrote a letter to the editor listing out the roughly 60 countries where homosexual sex was completely illegal, pointing out how parochial the Canadian debate on the subject was. Another letter writer, in the following issue of Capital Xtra, noted that several countries on my list were Muslim-majority countries, and that "the same homophobia" exists in "Christian" countries, therefore: "Is Islamophobia at play?"

The same kind of insinuations greeted the Conservative government's age-of-consent initiative, even though the law enjoyed all-party support (with the exception of the single vote of New Democratic Party MP Bill Siksay). Toronto queer activist Andrew Brett said gay teenagers should not be denied the right to have sex with grown men, and that the law was really about the Conservative governments' determination to "police the decisions of queer youth."

Brett was particularly furious that the NDP had agreed to the Conservatives' proposal, accusing party insiders of having "conspired" to squelch debate at the NDP's 2006 convention in Quebec City. The NDP had capitalized on its "slightly superior track record on issues such as same-sex marriage," Brett wrote, while at the same time "party apparatchiks are shamelessly working against the interest of queer party activists."

When Parliament finally raised the age of consent to 16 in 2008, Capital Xtra editor Gareth Kirkby was incensed. But not just with the Conservatives, from whom he expected such horrible behaviour, but with the Liberals and the New Democrats who voted with the government side, "even though artists and librarians, actors and playwrights, civil libertarians and gay activists begged them (and the Liberals) not to." The NDP was no better than the Liberals or the Conservatives, Kirkby protested, complaining that young gay people had been "abandoned" by NDP MPs, even those MPs known to be gay-friendly, and by NDP leader Jack Layton, and by the gay-friendly Liberal MP Hedy Fry and

Liberal Minister Bill Graham. He dismissed them all as prominent people who were happy to "wrap themselves in the rainbow flag for gay pride parades" one day and "sell out our youth" the next.

As for Prime Minister Stephen Harper and his Conservatives, Capital Xtra's descent into paranoid hysteria was so severe it could serve as evidence for Harper Derangement Syndrome qualifying for its own entry in the American Psychiatric Association's Diagnostic and Statistical Manual of Mental Disorders.

It began as soon as Harper was elected leader of the newly formed Conservative Party of Canada in March 2004, with Gareth Kirkby warning that "the Conservatives are a scary bunch," citing Harper's refusal to rule out the possibility that one of his MPs might introduce a private member's bill banning abortion. Right before the 2004 election, Associate Editor Julia Garro wrote that she was "freaking out a little bit over the possibility that the no-longer Progressive Conservatives will be forming the government after Monday's federal election. Prime Minister Stephen Harper? It's a frightening thought." In May, PTP Publisher David Walberg warned that while it was easy for Canadians to feel superior to Americans and the "moron" running their country, a "bigot and warlord," a "swashbuckling simpleton gunslinger" known for his "arrogant swagger, his ignorant words and the hokey drawl with which he mangles them," Stephen Harper, despite his "doughty face" and his appearance of "soft-hearted sensitivity," Canadians should be careful — very, very careful. "Conservatives may choose their words more carefully these days, but they remain the mean-spirited xenophobes they've always been."

After Harper lost to Liberal Prime Minister Paul Martin in the June 2004 election, columnist Blaine Marchand warned that Harper's Conservatives had merely pretended to be moderate, and that Canadians "need to remain suspicious of the muzzling of the Conservative party members and the apparent muting of the party's platform." If we weren't careful, the Conservatives would end up getting elected and then surprise everybody with "a type of government where decisions are made based on religious beliefs rather than for the protection, benefit and inclusion of all its citizens."

In March 2005, when the Conservatives held a policy convention in Montreal at which 25 per cent of the delegates voted to support same-sex marriage, Capital Xtra editor Gareth Kirkby had to admit that "the vitriol against gays, immigrants, bilingualism and social programs" that dominated conventions of the Conservatives' predecessor, the Reform Party, was absent. Still, Kirkby was bothered by the "radical set of right-wing policies" passed at the conference, among which he cited "raising the age of consent to 16" and "eliminating all defences against child porn."

Kirkby then went ballistic when Harper said "God Bless Canada" after a speech. "Monsignor Harper waits in the wings," Kirkby wrote, adding that "we'd better get ready for a battle for our rights that our opponents will cast in terms of biblical proportions. When God gets called into Parliament, he's seldom there to help the outcast."

But all this was all just a glimpse of the paranoia that was to come.

When the Conservatives won the election and Harper became prime minister in January 2006, even though only as the leader of a minority government, Capital Xtra went berserk. The cover story was headlined "Harper's Holy War On Homos."

Written by PTP Publisher David Walberg, the article set a new standard for shrillness. Canadians were about to be subjected to a "crusade," a rampage of fundamentalist Christianity and a subversion of multiculturalism to "mine the rich diversity of religious intolerance and make Canada a mosaic in the many hues of hate." The core Canadian values of social harmony, tolerance and mutual respect were going to be replaced with "a hodgepodge of the world's more regressive religious prejudices." Walberg likened Harper to an "an extreme Islamist" who goads the faithful against social permissiveness and decadence, "exploiting misunderstanding, fomenting bigotry, shredding the social fabric."

The idea that the Christian right had taken over Canada and was threatening to turn the whole country into an anti-gay, anti-feminist nightmare state wasn't confined to the pages of the Xtra newspapers, and it didn't subside even long after it was obviously untrue. In 2010, journalist Marci McDonald's book, *The Armageddon Factor: The Rise of Christian Nationalism in Canada*, was devoted entirely to the subject. McDonald's claim was that Harper's politics were "driven by a belief that Canada has a biblically ordained role to play in the final days before Armageddon and the Second Coming of Christ." Canadians had to "wake up to the fact that the political process is slowly being co-opted by an extremist vision of Christianity."

From 2006 on, in the Xtra newspapers, whenever the Conservatives were gay-friendly it was just a trick, a deception. If the Conservatives failed to fit the PTP/Xtra caricature, it was because they were hiding their true colours. If the Conservatives weren't obviously and openly waging a holy war on homos, it was only because they were putting it off to a more opportune moment. To PTP/Xtra, the facts didn't matter. The theory mattered. There was always a way to explain away the evidence that maybe the theory didn't hold water.

A few months after the Conservatives won the election, Conservative cabinet minister Michael Fortier attended the Outgames, formerly known as the Gay Olympics, in Montreal. He was there to formally welcome the athletes. When a chorus of boos went up, Capital Xtra's Ariel Troster was delighted to join in with the booing. "While the Conservatives might be intent on rolling back our human rights, this demonstrated that our community won't sit idly by while they do so. In fact, we're going to put up a fight. And this time, Fortier was on our turf."

In September, Capital Xtra columnist Brenda Crossman raised the spectre of Harper using his power of judicial appointments to have the Bible used to interpret the Constitution. Capital Xtra writer Marcus McCann continued in this vein, raising the fear that Harper could stack the courts with anti-gay and anti-abortion activists in order to allow conservative litigants to do an end-round around Parliament.

Before 2006 was over, Stephen Harper made good his promise to

have Parliament vote again on same-sex marriage, but he put absolutely
no energy into the motion and allowed only a day for debate. The Dec.
7 vote was 175-123 in favour of same-sex marriage, with six of Harper's
own cabinet members supporting the motion. Once the vote was over,
Harper told reporters: "I don't see reopening this question in the future."
But, rather than conceding that Harper's Conservatives were perhaps
not hell-bent on implementing a hidden anti-homo agenda after all,
Capital Xtra turned the event into evidence that Harper's Conservatives
had cunningly misled their own evangelical support base, and that
"in the end what it was really all about was Harper conning his own
constituency — religious conservatives — into voting for them." Even
so, same-sex marriage was no victory. It was just a "colonial imitation of
heterosexuality."

The truth is that social conservative issues were never really
important to Harper, an economist far more interested in such things
as international trade and developing the Alberta oil sands. If Xtra
had actually spoken with any actual Conservatives, they would have
had to confront that fact that, at least on social policy, Harper wasn't
particularly motivated by religious ideas at all. Neither he nor his
party were interested in pursuing anything like a "war on homos," holy
or otherwise. But Capital Xtra was not going to allow those facts to
contradict their theory or get in the way of any of their stories.

Several months after the end of the gay marriage debate in
Parliament, Marcus McCann wrote a massive essay for Capital Xtra:
"60 Reasons to dump Harper." Among these reasons: the Conservatives
should be expected to shut down the CBC and cut so far back on
cultural funding that it would put "hundreds of art fags out of work."
The hiring of a high-profile evangelical Christian by the Prime Minister's
Office meant: "It's time to move to Norway." Similarly terrifying was
Vancouver-Sunshine Coast EDA Conservative candidate John Weston,
who was known to lead "weekly devotionals at his law firm." Combine
Weston with the Roman Catholic cabinet minister Jason Kenney and
Sarnia, Ontario Conservative MP Cheryl Gallant, and gay people "could

be in a precarious position indeed." Reason No. 12: "Anti-sex PM targets strippers," referring to a federal effort to shut down a racket bringing Eastern European strippers into Canada. Other reasons gay people should be alarmed: "Harper remains 'personally opposed' to abortion," "safe injection sites could be in jeopardy," and "Harper criminalizes youth sexuality." That last one came with a warning that "we might have to fight against raising the age of consent to 18 soon."

Given Xtra's paranoid view of Canadian politics and its insistence that gay people remain in the category of the marginalized, their coverage of security and international affairs channeled Noam Chomsky, Norman Finkelstein, Haroon Siddiqui, and all the other 'blame America' and 'stick it to Israel' talking heads.

When Gareth Kirkby wrote in 2008 that Canadian troops should be brought home from Afghanistan, it was because our soldiers would "make things worse in the long-run" by fighting an unwinnable war that was putting Canada "at risk of blow-back violence by terrorists." The Afghan mission should be brought to an end because the Canadian sacrifice could not be said to have made things "permanently better" for women and gay people, human rights and a non-corrupt democracy. But that kind of "anti-war" posture had been a Pink Triangle hallmark from the beginning. Always two sides, with the West always the aggressor, and the "other side," which was assumed to include Muslim Canadians, always the party to be identified with.

During the Persian Gulf War in 1991, editorial commentary in Toronto's Xtra claimed that the war would "start with Iraqis, move on to anyone of Arab descent, then the dark-skinned, followed. . . by any dissenting voices, marginal and easy targets (that's us, girlfriend!)"

Blaine Marchand's first Capital Xtra column on international affairs after 9/11 begins with the question: "Do you feel threatened as a gay person?" Referring to an assault of a Muslim by white teenagers, Marchand wondered whether the recent turn of events would "spill over and target gays and lesbians." This theme continued in a November 2001 column by Pink Triangle board member Brenda Crossman about anti-terrorism legislation, which "should have us all concerned."

In April 2006, Ariel Troster wrote about the "modern day fight against terror where it's hard to separate the good guys from the bad ones."

Two months later, Troster was at it again. Canadians were vulnerable to terrorist reprisals because of a too-close association with the U.S. war on terror. Canada's contribution to the UN-authorized military mission in Afghanistan was merely "the logistical and material support that Canada is providing to the US occupation of Iraq," Gay people should choose sides. And not the side of Canada. Troster quotes an academic authority Xtra would routinely consult for party-line polemics in these matters, the Laurentian University professor Gary Kinsman: "If gays and lesbians have learned anything about our history, we should stand in solidarity with the people who are being targeted today."

Krishna Rau continued this theme in a double-page spread in November 2006. She went back to the ever-dependable Professor Kinsman, who claimed that anti-terror laws wouldn't be used only against terrorists, but could very well be used to target queers. Why would queers be targeted? Rau quotes Michael Vonn, policy director of the British Columbia Civil Liberties Association, saying that gay people could be "especially vulnerable to that kind of surveillance as they may use technology more than other groups." Kinsman was also worried that, although he hadn"t heard of any such cases, it was possible that security forces could force a gay Muslim to become an informant by threatening to out him.

The same spectre was said to haunt gay people in the United States. Matt Coles of the American Civil Liberties Union tells Rau that the war on terror was bound up in the Bush administration's religious agenda to target gays and lesbians. "The government that got us into Iraq is the same government that has been trying to promote a kind of religious orthodoxy. Terrorism and Iraq will be used as an excuse to centralize power and use it in part to advance a religious agenda."

In February 2015, Pink Triangle Press announced that the final editions of the Xtra newspapers were about to roll off the press, and that the venture was to continue in an online format only. PTP's David Walberg, wrote that the Xtra legacy amounted to four decades of championing sexual freedom and freedom of expression. "We hunger not for an equal slice of stale heterosexual pie, but for a heaping portion of sexual liberation, made to order from scratch."

Longtime Xtra contributor Mathew Hays wrote in the Globe and Mail that none of the progress that had been made could be taken for granted. The holy war could be just around the corner: "All it takes is for one election to provide us with politicians hostile to the idea of a rainbow flag in a public square, and we're back to square one. For those reasons it is imperative that we have a press for and by Canada's evolving queer communities."

The evangelical Christian coup never happened. But still, the end was nigh, or the war was always going on, or it was just about to break out. The Holy War on Homos was always, at the very least, an imminent threat that would surely erupt, at some point in the near-distant future.

By 2015, I'd already spent nine years in the enemy camp, and I'd never even heard any war drums. I found no anti-gay war rooms, and for most of those years, I'd been a completely "out" gay conservative. It wasn't as though there was no work to do: Conservatives needed to feel more comfortable with gay people, and the party needed to reach out to the gay community in the same way it was reaching out to ethnic groups. Building a network of gay conservatives was also going to be a useful project.

So that's what I set out to do.

Six

The Fabulous Blue Tent

At the November 2008 Conservative Party conference in Winnipeg, I launched Gay Dominion, a kind of club for gay conservatives, modelled after the Log Cabin Republicans in the United States. It was my first Conservative Party conference. I was there as a delegate for Ottawa Centre. I'd started my blog "GayandRight" three years earlier, and from the beginning, the reception from gay conservatives had been amazing. So why not establish something more formal right inside the conservative movement?

I set up a website and issued a press release: "Gay Dominion stands for limited government, low taxes, free markets, the merit principle, personal responsibility, AND the equality of gays and lesbians. Gay Dominion is against rampant political correctness, myopic religious intolerance, moral and cultural relativism, anti-Americanism, and the tearing down of western civilization."

There were no harsh reactions from any of the Conservative delegates I spoke with. The responses were mixed, and mainly on a spectrum between enthusiasm and indifference — but mostly indifference.

During a seminar by Citizenship and Immigration Minister Jason Kenney about outreach to ethnic and cultural groups (Kenney was also secretary of state for multiculturalism), I asked him when the gay community would be included in the party's outreach efforts. Kenney just shrugged and asked, what community is that? That was disappointing, but my only unpleasant encounter was during a later conversation with

Public Safety Minister Peter Van Loan, when I raised the same question that I'd put to Kenney. Van Loan looked puzzled, mumbled about there being a gay person in cabinet already (an obvious reference to John Baird, who was then Minister of Transport) and winked. I asked him: What on earth does that have to do with anything? He just scurried away.

There was obviously a lot of work that had to be done within the party. Conservatives had mostly moved on from tolerating antagonism to gays and lesbians, but the Conservative Party had yet to embrace the gay community.

The news media covering the convention weren't particularly interested in Gay Dominion — I got a few calls, but nothing substantial. It was hard to compete with all the news coming out of the conference. One of the bigger stories was a proposal to allow provinces to experiment with private health care. It was resoundingly defeated, following a stirring speech from Conservative MP Steven Fletcher, a paraplegic.

The only negative reaction to Gay Dominion came not from the right, but from the left — from John Baglow, that cranky former public-section union official whose blog, "Dr. Dawg," remained a repository for some of the most excessive "post-modern" leftism in Canada. Baglow was an accredited blogger at the conference. I'd spent a lot of time with him there, and went so far as to help him gather information about votes in sessions that the press was not allowed to attend. When I got back to Ottawa and noticed that none of his blog postings from the conference even mentioned Gay Dominion, I asked him why. He explained himself in an email: "It bothers me when I see gays; people of colour and so on attach themselves to a party whose ideological core is so antipathetic to who and what they are."

Just as I'd expected. Gays and people of colour are not allowed to be conservative.

Baglow clarified: "I don't expect all human beings to be ideologically coherent. There have even been Jews and Blacks who have reportedly joined the KKK, after all." When I asked him how he could compare me to a Jew joining the Ku Klux Klan, he protested: "Of course, I'm not comparing you to any such thing. . . surely you have noticed that homophobia is almost exclusively a right-wing phenomenon? The cluster of values that defines 'conservatism' is not very friendly to non-het orientations." He seemed taken aback when I told him that gay people did not always fare well in left-wing regimes, and that in Cuba, gay people were persecuted, and routinely imprisoned.

I ended up getting lots of emails from gay people about Gay Dominion, and for a while I thought about putting on a conference in Toronto. But I just didn't have enough energy to build a national organization while I also worked on NorthernBlues and the Free Thinking Film Society. It's one thing to show a film in Ottawa. It's quite another to organize a cross-Canada conference.

But persuading Canada's conservative establishment to actively embrace the gay community was going to require some hard work, I figured. This was plainly evident at the March 2009 Manning Centre Networking Conference and Exhibition in Ottawa.

The Manning Centre had been established in Calgary in 2005 by Preston Manning, the former leader of the populist and social conservative Reform Party. By 2009, the Manning Centre was hosting an annual conference in Ottawa. There were speeches, panel discussions and exhibitions of other conservative think tanks and non-governmental organizations. At the 2009 event, there was a presentation on the campaign in California to overturn Proposition 8, a ballot initiative from the previous year to institute a constitutional ban on same-sex marriage. The campaign won by a 52-48 percentage margin. Campaign organizer Frank Schubert was in there to talk about his strategies and tactics. I was dismayed.

I was nervous attending, but I wanted to see for myself what Schubert might say. The talk was supposed to be about campaign strategy, and I was hoping there would be minimal talk about same-sex marriage and gay people. But that was not to be. There was a lot of snickering at certain points in Schubert's talk, including from the

Manning Centre's representative at the seminar, Richard Ciano. At one point, Schubert went so far as to say there was no scientific data to show that homosexuality was an inherent trait. He also claimed that same-sex marriage had lowered marriage rates in Canada, but, in fact, marriage rates were declining long before gay marriage was legalized in this country. Was Schubert also an expert on Canadian matrimonial trends?

After the presentation, I complained to Ciano, and all he could say was he didn't know if homosexuality was inherent or a "learned" trait. Then he said there was going to be some balance in the morning seminars because the next session, on how to conduct focus groups, was to be conducted by Jaime Watt — a prominent Canadian gay conservative and the initiator of the Equal Marriage Initiative within Canada's conservative movement. I was aghast. How could these two seminars balance out? Watt wasn't going to rebut Schubert on marriage. He was going to talk about focus groups. His sexual orientation was irrelevant. When I raised the issue of the snickering and laughing during Schubert's talk, Ciano said that I was patronizing him, and like Peter Van Loan had done, he ran away. Later, when I spoke with Watt about Schubert's seminar, he said that he was outraged that Schubert had been invited. Watt had steered clear of the seminar, preferring to lay low in his hotel room.

I wrote a letter of complaint to the Manning Centre, detailing exactly what had happened. What I wanted to know was whether the Manning Centre wanted to re-open the same-sex marriage issue in Canada (at the conclusion of Schubert's seminar there had a been a show-of-hands vote on the question, and most people voted "yes"). Most of the questions following Schubert's presentation were about same-sex marriage, not campaign strategy. Why bring in Schubert in the first place? In my letter I warned that reviving the social conservative crusade against same-sex marriage would lead only to a "small-tent" conservative movement and a return to years of Liberal rule. I concluded: "I wonder whether your tent is big enough for gay people and their spouses as well as the Churches, Synagogues and other institutions that support them."

I waited for about six weeks for an answer. Nothing. I then emailed Stephen Taylor, a technology consultant and founder of Blogging Tories; he was a prominent person in Manning Centre circles. Within days, I received a reply from Preston Manning. He apologized that same-sex marriage had become such a focus of the Schubert session, which was supposed to have been about campaign organization and technology. "I am sorry if that became more of a focus than it should have," Manning wrote, adding that the conservative movement "should be big enough to include all Canadians who subscribe to conservative principles."

It's worth noting here that Jaime Watt — the Manning Centre's idea of "balance" against the Schubert seminar, merely because Watt happens to be gay — is a gay conservative hero. Watt was responsible for Bill 5, a 1999 Ontario law that extended to same-sex couples the same rights and responsibilities as heterosexual common-law couples. Bolstered by a Supreme Court ruling, Watt almost singlehandedly forced the bill through Mike Harris's Conservative government, overcoming some powerful initial resistance.

Watt went on to pioneer the Canadians for Equal Marriage campaign within Canada's conservative movement, which had helped open the doors for my own Gay Dominion effort. Watt, too, was subjected to abuse from the left for his efforts. In 2009, when Watt was presented with a leadership award from EGALE, the gay human rights group, Capital Xtra's editorialists were incensed. Under the headline "Gay Leaders denounce EGALE Award to Jaime Watt," prominent Toronto bathhouse owner Peter Bochove is reported saying: "I'm sorry, that's just wrong. I find it personally offensive. I don't understand how you can be gay and belong to these parties. . . It's the antithesis of everything in the gay community."

The Conservatives didn't exactly help their cause that year when they took a tourism program away from Diane Ablonczy, Minister of State for Tourism, after she gave $400,000 to the Toronto Pride parade. And the following year, the Conservative government ended funding for the Toronto Pride parade and the Montreal Gay Arts Festival as well.

The government denied any anti-gay bias was involved, and that it was a simple matter of Toronto getting too big a piece of the subsidy pie, and that a greater diversity of projects needed to be funded. The appearance of bias was there, nonetheless.

While I was working away to make the Conservative Party more openly gay-friendly, I hadn't given up entirely on the effort to make the gay press more open to gay conservatives. But that was a much tougher slog.

Back in March 2006, I'd asked Capital Xtra editor Gareth Kirkby whether he'd be interested in a gay conservative column. Some gay newspapers in the United States had added conservative columnists, and Andrew Sullivan was making a name for himself in the U.S. as a gay conservative author and blogger. I asked Kirkby whether his concern for diversity extended to diversity of political thought in the gay community. Kirkby replied that he was not looking for an ongoing column by a gay conservative, but that I could write a one-off opinion piece. I suggested an article pointing out the Islamist threat to gay people, not in Muslim-majority countries, but in liberal European cities like Amsterdam. But he turned me down, saying that he already had a "package" coming in on that topic.

I then suggested a column on the lack of diversity of thought in the gay media. He turned that down, too, saying it was unnecessary: "Have you seen the columns we run? Local issues, like the community centre, the gaybourhood, school safety. Our columns are local people writing about making their immediate environment better for themselves and their friends and community."

Yes, except all those articles about Stephen Harper, George Bush, Afghanistan and Iraq and so on. When I met with Kirkby two months later, he told me the real reason a column of the kind I was proposing was impossible was that Capital Xtra had a left-wing mandate set by the directors at Pink Triangle Press. I would simply not fit with their mission.

I'd hoped things might have changed a little after Kirkby left, and Marcus McCann took over as Capital Xtra's editor. At first, things looked promising.

In 2009, I brought gay American author Bruce Bawer to Ottawa to speak on his new book, *Surrender: Appeasing Islam, Sacrificing Freedom*. Bawer had written more than 10 books, and his 1993 book, *A Place at the Table: The Gay Individual in America Society,* was one the most influential books ever written on homosexuality, and was a New York Times Notable Book of the Year. Bawer had also contributed hundreds of articles and reviews to publications as diverse as the New York Times, the Washington Post, the Wall Street Journal, City Journal, the New Republic, the Cato Policy Report and The Nation. Surrender contains a chapter, "Selling Out the Sodomites" on the intolerance to gay people in the Muslim world and the increasingly hostility to gays exhibited by Muslim communities in western countries. I'd thought that bringing him to Ottawa would be an important event for the gay community, particularly since Bawer had been a longtime champion of gay rights.

I booked an appointment to see McCann, expecting that he'd not only publicize Bawer's speech, but would also help arrange a private breakfast with Bawer and various gay community leaders in Ottawa. McCann agreed to help. I thought this was a big breakthrough.

But the next time I spoke to McCann, he'd clearly had a change of heart. He claimed he didn't know any gay leaders in Ottawa, and in any event, he'd be on holiday when Bawer was in town. And no reporter from Capital Xtra would be sent to cover Bawer's speech, either. I was genuinely surprised. I also asked Alex Munter, a prominent gay politician who was popular in Capital Xtra's pages (Munter had run unsuccessfully for mayor of Ottawa in 2006) whether he'd be at least interested in meeting Bruce. Munter said he was too busy. But he did send me this note to pass on to Bruce:

"As both a candidate for office and in my work on the equal marriage campaign, my experience has been that right-of-centre politicians in Canada have deliberately stoked anti-gay sentiment wherever they could find it, including in minority communities, in order to achieve their political goals. I would have been interested to hear Bruce's take on that so I am sorry to miss the opportunity."

Not a horrible question, but deliberately provocative and obviously unrelated to the topic of Bruce's speech.

In the end, there was no meeting between Bawer and Ottawa's gay leaders. Capital Xtra's sole contribution was to include Bruce's speech in the newspaper's event listings, omitting any reference to the subject of the speech. Otherwise, it was a hugely successful event.

In the meantime, the Conservatives had made the decision to reach out to the gay community. I heard it firsthand from Jason Kenney, the cabinet minister I'd spoken with about the subject at the 2008 party conference in Winnipeg.

In June of 2010, I hosted a dinner at my house for Bat Ye'or, the outspoken Jewish-Egyptian author who'd coined the term "Eurabia" and was highly critical of the influence of the Organization of the Islamic Conference at the United Nations. Kenney agreed to attend the dinner because he was an avid reader of Bat Ye'or's books, but disputed Ye'or's argument about the OIC's significance. The highlight of the evening was Kenney's spirited rebuttal, in fluent French, on the grounds that the OIC was too fragmented and too conflicted to agree on anything like a new caliphate.

When the evening was over, Jason pulled me aside and told me he was reaching out to bring gay Iranian refugees into Canada. He was also hoping the gay community could help by sponsoring more people. The following month, in Vancouver, Kenney convened a meeting on the Private Sponsorship of Refugees (PSR) program. The attendees included a variety of church groups as well as the Rainbow Refugee Committee. Kenney announced that a refugee reform package would include a 20 per cent hike in refugee resettlement, and he wanted the gay community to get organized and participate. He also said he would be meeting with other LGBT communities across the country.

This was huge.

The government was going to bring in more gay refugees, and it was actively trying to engage with the LGBT community. This should have been a cause for celebration, but the event was hardly noticed. It just didn't fit with the overall left-wing derangement on Afghanistan, Iraq and the war on terror, and it stood as a rebuke to the hysteria about Harper's Holy War on Homos that had come to dominate international commentary in the gay press.

In light of all that, it should not be surprising that anti-Israel animus was creeping into that most unlikely of places — Gay Pride in Toronto.

Queers Against Israeli Apartheid (QuAIA) was a gay activist group formed after the 2008 Israel Apartheid Week in Toronto (Canada is the birthplace of the world's many annual "Israel apartheid week" goings-on). Israel is a bastion of gay rights — with gays actively serving in the military, gay pride marches in Tel Aviv and Jerusalem, and state recognition of same-sex marriages. There is also an underground network to bring gay Palestinians who are being threatened to Israel.

All of this makes it hard to protest Israel, you would think, so QuAIA had to make up something, and settled on a complaint about "the use of gay rights as a propaganda tool to justify Israel's apartheid policies." A coalition was necessary "to fight against this appropriation." Thus QuAIA was born, and the term "pinkwashing," invented in Toronto, entered the international anti-Zionist vocabulary.

There is rich irony in all this. The gay movement establishment in Canada, and particularly its official media — the Pink Triangle Press newspapers — had become overtly hostile to the forces involved in the ongoing advance of gay rights, gay inclusion and acceptance of gay people. Its derangement was occurring right at the time that gay people were being most warmly and openly welcomed by the gay establishment's erstwhile enemies — the Conservative Party, the courts, the legislatures and every other "heterosexist" institution in the country. The very last thing a gay activist would want to do is to notice any of the glaring contradictions in the gay establishment "narrative," however.

In the summer of 2010, when I was looking for documentaries for the first Annual Free Thinking Film Festival, I came across *Reclaiming Pride* by Toronto lawyer and musician Martin Gladstone. It was about Queers Against Israeli Apartheid, specifically about the controversy around the inclusion of QuAIA in the 2009 Toronto Gay Pride parade.

I knew that I wanted to show it at the festival. I also figured it would stir things up, which made the film even more appealing to me. And it sure stirred things up, a lot more than I'd anticipated.

The *Reclaiming Pride* film builds the case that QuAIA's inclusion in the parade violated the guidelines governing the grant funding (exceeding $400,000) the Toronto Pride was receiving from the City of the Toronto and the Ontario provincial government — specifically Toronto's discrimination and racism prohibitions and the city's access and equity policies. As a nonprofit dedicated to celebrating gay rights, issues outside Toronto Pride's mandate are out of bounds. During the parade, participants must show support for the gay community at large and are not allowed to promote hatred or negative stereotypes of any group. QuAIA's inadmissibility should have been obvious just by its slogan: "Fist by fist, blow by blow, apartheid state has got to go."

Gladstone should have realized that logic and reason would get him nowhere. Ultimately, the city's director of equity, diversity and human rights, Uzma Shakir, wrote in a 2012 report that the term Israeli apartheid did not violate Toronto's anti-discrimination policies. It turned out that Shakir was a regular contributor to Rabble.ca, the media sponsor of Israel Apartheid Week. Indeed, Shakir had written an opinion piece criticizing Jason Kenney's decision to defund the Canadian Arab Federation, and in her bio on the University of Windsor website, where she was a distinguished visitor in Women's Studies, she wrote that "Western feminists want to 'save' Afghan women, Muslim women from themselves, rather than focus their critiques on the actions of men such as Stephen Harper and George Bush, whose policies have terrible consequences for the lives of Afghan and Muslim women."

The first hint that *Reclaiming Pride* was going to cause trouble came as soon as I'd announced that it was going to be shown in the Free

Thinking film festival. Jeremy Dias, the founder and executive director of Jer's Vision, a charity that works to eradicate bullying in high schools (Dias had written articles for the gay press about "queering" campuses, and also about "Israeli apartheid") was miffed that I'd included him on the email list I'd developed to promote the film. He accused me of "promoting discrimination" just by choosing to show the film.

I had no idea what he was talking about, so I asked him. He said I should do my research, by reading Capital Xtra, and that the film had been "doctored" and contained many inaccuracies.

This was the first I'd heard about these allegations. It turned out that the allegations were groundless, but they had been circulated by Capital Xtra. The "doctoring" claim was that Gladstone had distorted QuAIA's chants during the parade, and muffled supporting cheers from the crowds as the QuAIA contingent passed by.

A week after Dias took me to task, the Ottawa Police Gay Liaison Committee was blasted in an article and an editorial in Capital Xtra. All the liaison committee had done was pass on my email promoting the film through its own email list. In the article, Dias is quoted saying the Ottawa Police were being "not just offensive and insulting and embarrassing," but were also showing that the police had "no idea about the community they are working in." QuAIA's Tim McCaskell told Capital Xtra that the Ottawa Police Gay Liaison Committee "shouldn't be promoting that kind of political agenda." In Capital Xtra's editorial on the subject, editor Marcus McCann accused the Ottawa Police of promoting the film, the showing of which threatened to "kick off a Pride Toronto-calibre meltdown in Ottawa."

Just one irony was that all the Ottawa Police had done was to forward an email about a film on a gay-activism theme, but this was wrong because — according to Dias — the goal of the police gay liaison committee was to "allow or to encourage a space for critical thinking, critical dialogue and solution-finding." The chutzpah: Dias and McCaskell demanded that the Ottawa Police apologize.

The showing of Gladstone's *Reclaiming Pride* was uneventful. The first annual Free Thinking Film Festival had been a roaring success. And while Ottawa's gay establishment was busy closing itself off from any real "critical thinking, critical dialogue and solution-finding," my work to open up the Conservative Party to gay people was being met with enthusiasm. The big breakthrough was the Fabulous Blue Tent. What a party!

The idea came from my friend Jamie Ellerton, a former aide to Jason Kenney. Jamie wanted to throw a party for gay conservatives and their friends at the upcoming June 2011 Conservative Party conference in Ottawa. He invited me and my friend Roy Eappen from the Film Society board into the planning group. We set out to raise funds by having a little fun and asking people to "join the friends of Dorothy and their sisters at The Fabulous Blue Tent." We didn't mention gay people explicitly, but the term "friend of Dorothy" made it clear to most people. The term dates back to the movie The Wizard of Oz and World War II, when it was a way to discreetly talk about sexual orientation. Of course, Judy Garland ultimately became a gay icon. To some conservatives, the invitation was still a little opaque. I remember riding the elevator up to our suite during the Conservative Party conference and overhearing some delegates trying to figure out what the term meant.

We'd raised enough money to not just to pay for free booze but to offer delegates several choices of wine. Our exquisite suite at the Westin Hotel came with a huge patio balcony for more than 100 people (we even hired a DJ) and The Fabulous Blue Tent ended up being easily the best party at the conference. Two cabinet ministers (Kenney and John Baird, who'd just been appointed foreign affairs minister) and several MPs attended. Nearly 600 people showed up. The party lasted into the wee hours of the morning, and there was a lot of press attention, with mentions in Maclean's magazine, the Toronto Star and the National Post.

Even Capital Xtra allowed a favourable mention of the event to appear in its pages. But Xtra's paranoid hostility soon re-emerged, after the suicide of Jamie Hubley, the son of Ottawa city councillor Allan

Hubley, in October that year.

Jamie Hubley was only 15. He'd been suffering from depression and had been the victim of anti-gay bullying at school. Several Conservative MPs, senators and cabinet ministers produced a short YouTube video, called It Gets Better, aimed at lifting the spirits of gay teenagers suffering from bullying and to raise awareness about the anti-bullying Kids Helpline. Instead of welcoming the initiative, Capital Xtra published an "open letter" to Prime Minister Stephen Harper by Xtra freelancer Rob Salerno, who complained that the video "falls flat" because the Conservative politicians involved were "not the greatest champions of gay people." Salerno took particular exception to Baird's appearance in the video, because while Baird had been "outed" as gay the year before, he had chosen to keep his sexuality a private matter. "Having Baird in the video," Salerno wrote, "is almost like saying, 'It gets better as long as you never, ever tell anyone you're gay.'"

Baird's refusal to make a big deal about his sexuality ended up being a regular Capital Xtra complaint, even while the newspaper was going out of its way to publish photographs of Baird at Ottawa's Gay Pride parade after-party. Personally, I would have preferred it if Baird had formally come out of the closet and talked openly about being gay. But that was his choice to make, and throughout his career he had always been supportive of gay rights — he'd twice voted in Parliament to support same-sex marriage and he'd gone on to become Canada's most outspoken foreign minister on the subject of gay rights internationally. When Baird decided to move on from politics and return to private life in February 2015, Opposition foreign affairs critic Paul Dewar, of the NDP, praised Baird as having "led like no other minister on the world stage when it came to the persecution of gays, lesbians and transsexuals."

If you relied on the Xtra newspapers, you'd probably be shocked to learn that the Conservative government had been standing up for gay people since at least 2009. In November that year, at a Commonwealth meeting in Trinidad, Stephen Harper spoke out about Uganda's attempt to pass harsh anti-gay laws. The Commonwealth was the forum where Harper's government hoped to make some real international progress on gay rights. In January 2012, Baird gave a speech to the Royal Commonwealth Society in London blasting the "dozens" of Commonwealth countries that maintained regressive and punitive laws criminalizing homosexuality. "Throughout most of the Commonwealth Caribbean, colonial-era laws remain on the books that could impose draconian punishments on gay people simply for being gay," Baird noted. He referred as well to a law Russia had just adopted (the law banned the so-called "promotion of homosexuality") that was as backwards as the laws still on the books of Commonwealth member states. Canada had sent a letter of protest to Moscow about it and placed a cautionary travel advisory on his department's foreign-travel web page.

But Baird's contribution was only one of many examples of the way the Harper government was finding its feet on LGBT issues. Jason Kenney was taking extraordinary steps forward in his policies as immigration minister and in his public pronouncements. In November 2011, in a speech to a conference of the UN High Commission for Refugees, Kenney drew close attention to gay and lesbian refugees and the threats they faced. In a September 2012 statement, Kenney said: "Canada should always be a place of refuge for those who truly need our protection. That is why we continue to welcome those fleeing persecution, which oftentimes includes certain death, including on the basis of sexual orientation." Kenney noted that the government had boosted the resettlement of gay refugees into Canada, and had reached out particularly to Iran's persecuted gay community, and was working with Canadian groups such as the Rainbow Refugee Committee to help them sponsor gay refugees.

But no good Conservative deed was going to go unpunished. Kenney had committed the disgraceful indiscretion of releasing his September 2012 statement in an email sent to Canadians who had previously petitioned his office on gay rights issues. Xtra's Ariel Troster complained to the Ottawa Citizen that Kenney's letter was an eruption of "homonationalism." The Citizen quoted York University student Johannah May Black (an activist in York's Students Against Israeli Apartheid group) calling the letter an outbreak of "pinkwashing" that exposed the Conservative government's "obvious desire to encourage war with Iran." In his full-page letter, Kenney had mentioned Iran in a single, passing reference. Further, the refugee record for 2011 shows that Canada had accepted 762 refugees on the basis of their sexual orientation from more than 90 countries.

Capital Xtra was similarly apoplectic, reporting that Kenney's "creepy" letter had left its recipients "scratching their heads how the ministry got a list of emails for queer Canadians." In a response to Xtra, Kenney noted that the letter's recipients were drawn from the earlier petition they'd sent to his office. "I've been in Parliament for 15 years and I've never seen a more ridiculous reaction to an issue than people objecting to being corresponded with by a parliamentarian's office after having contacted that office on that issue with their email address." For his trouble, Kenney was asked by Xtra whether he was gay. A Roman Catholic, Kenney refused to answer, saying his sexuality was a personal matter (the idea that Kenney was gay was widespread, and while I neither knew nor cared, he appeared to be living his life celibate).

In that same article, Sharalyn Jordan of the Rainbow Refugee Committee (part of a small group of organizations that Kenney had funded to the tune of $100,000 to help them resettle the gay refugees he had encouraged to come to Canada) also dismissed Kenney's letter as "pinkwashing," adding that it was "a blatant attempt to create a negative shift in public opinion towards Iran by highlighting the homophobia faced by queer people there."

The following year, even John Baird's outspoken condemnation of Vladimir Putin's anti-gay laws in Russia had Capital Xtra complaining: "Come out of the closet if you want to help Russian gays, activists tell Baird." The article made it appear as though an August 2013 demonstration and march in Toronto was not so much to protest Moscow's persecution of Russia's gay people, but to protest that Baird could not be effective in his opposition to Moscow's anti-gay bigotry unless he "came out" as a gay man.

Once again, the gay community was proving itself increasingly impossible to work with, even as the Conservative government, along with both "small c" and "large C" conservatives, was becoming increasingly open and welcoming of homosexuality and of gay people.

There were pockets of hostility, of course, like the anti-feminist REAL Women organization. REAL Women opposed John Baird's 2013 funding of a gay group in Uganda that was fighting a law stipulating the death penalty for homosexuals and REAL Women also protested Baird's continued campaign against Russia's anti-gay laws. But the REAL Women outfit was finding itself isolated and condemned by almost every group within the conservative movement. There were also the far-right corners of the Canadian blogosphere, like Kathy Shaidle of Five Feet of Fury. In January 2010, Shaidle lampooned Ugandan gay activists by referring to a BBC report on witch doctors and child sacrifice in Uganda: "Who cares about little kids being tortured and killed — we want butt sex." But these were aberrations. The conservative landscape in Canada, once so hostile to gay people, was in a state of radical transformation.

It had gotten so that a National Post article in September 2012 ran with the headline: "Warriors for Gay Rights: The Conservatives have become unlikely LGBT supporters" The subhead: "How Canada's Conservative Party has become a champion of gay rights." And in July 2013, Vice.com ran a story with the headline: "Is Canada Run by a Gay Mafia?" The National Post article documented the many advances for gay people under the Conservative government (I was quoted saying, "I can no longer shock people in the conservative movement when I tell them that I'm gay — but I can shock gay people by telling them I'm Conservative.") and laid out the obvious evidence against the popular conspiracy theory that the Conservatives were harbouring an "anti-gay hidden agenda." The Vice.com article, which was purposely over the top, claimed "Canada's Conservative party appears to be run by a queer mafia that rivals the Vatican."

By 2014, the colourful conservative media personality Michael Coren, an old-style Roman Catholic and a longtime opponent of gay rights, was confessing in an opinion piece in the Toronto Sun headlined "I was wrong" that his views have evolved on the subject of homosexuality. "I can no longer hide behind comfortable banalities, have realized that love triumphs judgement, and know that the conversation between Christians and gays has to transform — just as, to a large extent, the conversation between conservatives and gays has."

Even in the United States, the evangelical Christian community was reconsidering its attitudes. By early 2015, the Public Religion Research Institute published a survey that found that 42 per cent of young evangelicals supported same-sex marriage. Also in 2015, the Mormons announced that they would "pledge to support anti-discrimination laws for gays, lesbians, bisexuals and transgender people, as long as the laws also protect the rights of religious groups." A few weeks later, the State of Utah passed a law prohibiting discrimination against LGBT people. The law was supported by the Mormon Church.

We held a second Fabulous Blue Tent event in November 2013 at the national Conservative Party convention in Calgary. Prime Minister Harper's wife Laureen attended for several hours while the party raged. It was so crowded that it was hard to be certain, but at least six cabinet ministers and at least 10 MPs attended. We were turning people away. We were no longer referring to ourselves as Friends of Dorothy, but instead explicitly invited gay conservatives and their friends. We presented an award to the government for its work in promoting gay rights around the world; the award was accepted by Chris Alexander, who had taken over the immigration portfolio from Kenney, who'd moved on to his new cabinet portfolio in employment and social development. The CBC covered the event. Headlined "Fabulous blue tent showcases gay Conservatives' power," the CBC report noted that our event was "the party everyone wanted to go to" at the convention and that a person couldn't get in unless someone else was leaving.

All of this should have made Xtra and the gay leadership ecstatic. But no. Instead of heralding progress, the gay movement establishment was retreating even further into the weird, Foucault-inflected recesses of postmodernism.

In January of 2013, a Capital Xtra inquiry into the progress of gay normalization and integration led readers to the depressing conclusion that the phenomenon was a betrayal of the progressive gay cause. In that article, condemning the "emergence of the neoliberal queer," sociologist Gary Kinsman (who by 2015 had retired and was working on a book to be titled *The Making of the Neo-Liberal Queer)* offered two ways to dismiss gay integration. It was either a submission to "homonormativity," which is a dreary middle-class "normalness," or it was "homonationalism," which was just as bad, because it would encourage lesbians and gay men to "identify with their nation state as the liberator of queer people and how gay rights and women's rights have been deployed to justify the war in Afghanistan, the occupation in Iraq, and Western opposition to the Palestinian struggle for self-determination." The article was partly to promote two of Kinsman's upcoming seminars. One, at York University, was titled "Queering Heterosexism in the Social Form of Legal and State Formation: National Security and Homonationalism." The other Kinsman seminar, to be convened at the University of Toronto, was titled "The Making of the Neoliberal Queer: Class, Race, Homonormativity and Homonationalism."

As noted in the previous chapter of this book, Kinsman was an authority Xtra routinely consulted for ideological guidance. It was Kinsman who was telling Capital Xtra in 2006 that gay people should identify with the "targets" of Canada's military engagement in Afghanistan, lest gay people fall prey to the "homonationalism" of identifying too closely with Canada and with "heteronormative" Canadians. Here it was, seven years later, and the progress gay people had witnessed by 2013 was not progress at all. There was still "the heterosexist terror that young people face on the streets and schools."

As for addressing the bullying problem, a project like that was pretty hopeless, Kinsman said, because high schools remained "training grounds for the reproduction of hegemonic heterosexual masculinity in society. We're not getting at the social roots of violence."

By 2015, Kinsman was writing his book about neoliberal queers and running his personal website (Radical Noise!) inspired by the Zapatista movement of southern Mexico and "the rip they have made in the fabric of capitalist and oppressive social relations," as well as "direct action anti-poverty organizing, anti-racist feminism, the global and climate justice movements, and more recently the Occupy movement and Idle No More." The website was devoted to "anti-capitalist and anti-oppression politics and to struggles for queer liberation" and drew from "the red threads within autonomist Marxism."

With queer icons like Kinsman, it was no wonder that Capital Xtra would run an article like Adam Graham's February 2004 contribution, arguing that "crack pipes are a queer issue." Gay people were reported to need crack pipes more than straight people because some studies showed that queer youth were eight times more likely to be crackheads. I don't know if this is true or not, but it seems the solution is not more crack pipes. Going by Kinsman's guidance, it shouldn't be surprising that Ariel Troster could write an February 2008 opinion piece titled "Sex work. Our Struggle."

In a July 2011 double-page spread, Capital Xtra's Marcus McCann set out the "unfinished project of gay activism" that listed the 25 battles "still being fought." These included providing a safe labour environment for sex workers, rescinding Canada's anti-polygamy laws, "empowering youth in their sexuality," eliminating gender from government identification and forms," extending provincial health insurance to include sex reassignment surgery across Canada, scaling back on state surveillance, "breaking down hetero assumptions about parenting," and "broadening representations of gay and trans people in mainstream media." It was only at No. 22 that the spread gets around to "promoting queer and human rights abroad." And that was in small print at the bottom of the page.

Finally. An acknowledgement that we have to help our brothers and sisters overseas. But this had always been close to the lowest possible priority for the gay movement leadership in Canada. We were to focus on the perpetually unfinished liberationist agenda at home, which by Kinsman's standards was pretty well an unachievable goal anyway. Better to focus on slaying the homegrown dragons of homonationalism and heteronormativity than to be concerned with something like the brutal persecution and criminalization of gay people elsewhere. Unless of course it meant battling Israel wherever possible.

In 2014, Canada's gay community had a golden opportunity to show some leadership in promoting gay rights internationally when Toronto was chosen as the host city for the international celebration WorldPride. But the opportunity was wasted.

Doug Kerr, co-chair of the WorldPride human rights conference, told attendants at a QuAIA Pride Week event in 2013 in Toronto that he was worried that WorldPride could become "an orgy of pinkwashing." Ali Abunimah, co-founder of the anti-Israel "Electronic Intifada" and a proponent of the one-state solution (code for the destruction of the State of Israel), then asserted that the Canadian government was "one of the worst offenders in perpetuating pinkwashing" on Israel's behalf. At the seminar, Kerr told Abunimah that "many of us involved in organizing see it [WorldPride] as an opportunity for social justice education," and, of course, that would mean making "pinkwashing" a central issue.

The following year in Vancouver, the directors of two films withdrew their entries in the 2014 Vancouver Queer Film Festival because a local Jewish group had combined an Israeli flag with a Pride flag in a $630 sponsorship advertisement the group had bought in the festival's guidebook. One of the film directors, Patty Berne, said the advertisement was unacceptably offensive because it presented Israel "as a friend to LGBTQ communities" at a time when "the people of Palestine are living through hell and dying in staggering numbers daily" (the film festival coincided with Israel's Operation Protective Edge in

Gaza).

The sad fact is that Xtra was far more interested in helping QuAIA as much as possible. In 2011, when there was a change in the leadership at Toronto Gay Pride, Susan G. Cole, lesbian author and activist, wrote in Xtra that "I don't care how powerful the Jewish community is in Toronto, no way a first-time filmmaker like Martin Gladstone should have had so much more impact on the issue than a smart leader of Pride who understood how to protect the festival's interests."

So, it's the Jews who are ruining Gay Pride?

In the eight years of Xtra newspapers that I surveyed in detail, I found a paltry four articles about international gay rights in the heaps of articles about "queer theory," about how gay people should storm into straight bars to take over heteronormative spaces, about the development of a "new vision of lesbian identity" called Deep Lez, and think pieces pondering "the right kind of porn" for men, or fretting about the dangers implicit in prosecuting dissident Mormon polygamists in British Columbia. Was the "hypothetical lesbian household" in danger? Were women secretly thinking there was "something abnormal about their pussies"? Had the long history of nudism at Pride "taught spectators to expect it"? Shouldn't non-transsexuals be required to "acknowledge cisgender privilege"?

Here's an unasked question: Why has the mainstream media not reported on what has been going on in the gay community? Perhaps the straight media was scared of being accused of heterosexism by or homophobia for even inquiring into such matters.

In September of 2014, I was a guest on Steve Paikin's TVO program "The Agenda" with the topic "Of Rainbows and Democracy." Some of the questions examined were, "What does it mean to be gay around the world in the 21st century? To what extent does acceptance of homosexuality and same-sex marriage stand as a litmus test for progression? Why do we see a progressive shift in countries like Canada, and a negative shift in countries like Russia?" These were all very good questions.

I argued strenuously that it was time to do a little less partying and a little more hard work, that the gay community should begin to focus on international issues, and that it was a problem that the issue of Israel had taken all the oxygen out of the discussion. Andrea Houston, journalist and assistant to Ontario NDP MPP Cheri Dinovo, disagreed and launched into a diatribe about "pinkwashing" homophobia at home, and this: "We as queer people stand in solidarity with sex workers." It all went downhill from there. The other three panellists were of the same mind as Houston. I'd been such a discordant voice that after the show, they wouldn't even let me share their taxi from the studio.

By 2015, Canada's gay establishment, having already lost all sense of proportion, had retreated deep into the comfortable politics that the American writer Andrew Sullivan described in his book, *Virtually Normal*, as a "strange confluence of political abdication and psychological violence." There was no real leadership at all. There are gay bars, but no credible organizations, just a never-ending mobilization that had nowhere to go. Gay people were being executed in places like Iran, and we were marching in assless chaps. Gay people have no absolutely no rights and no legal protection in large parts of the world, but we were concerned with crack pipes, "twincest" pornography, whether there is some other letter to add at the end of LGBTQ, and how much sex workers should be charging for their services. We condemn Israel, the only truly gay-friendly country in the Middle East, but point out the persecution of gay people in Muslim-majority countries and you will be written off as a pinkwashing homonationalist. While jihadists were throwing gay men from the roofs of tall buildings in Iraq and Syria, we were condemning western society for its hostile heteronormativity. We were sneering at heterosexuals, calling them breeders, and then demanding that heterosexuals treat us with deference and respect.

A few days after Xtra shut down their print editions, QuAIA disbanded and said they would no longer march in Gay Pride. Tim McCaskell, one of QuAIA's founding members, said that "It wasn't an easy decision to make. But we decided that retiring QuAIA allows us all to develop new strategies for supporting the Palestine solidarity movement and to make new links across oppressions in our communities." The irony is touching — McCaskell and his merry band of Israel-bashers have subjugated the gay community for years with their empty debates on freedom of speech and their insistence that "Israeli apartheid" be a proper rallying cry for a festival.

Ali Abunimah, of the Electronic Intifada, said that "QuAIA's work provided an important political analysis that has educated me and many others about what principled solidarity looks like." He's got it totally backwards. It's the Harper Conservative government who is teaching the community about 'principled solidarity' — not Pink Triangle Press, not Xtra newspapers, not QuAIA, and not Toronto Pride.

Yes, it took a few years longer for conservatives to come onside than liberals. But, when will the gay leadership start to care about our brothers and sisters across the globe? Isn't it ironic that a Conservative Canadian government talks more about gay rights internationally than the gay community itself?

Seven

You Need a Documentary for That?

It was a cool November morning in 2011 and Andrew and I were attending a conference on the delegitimization of Israel in Montreal. The Canadian Institute for Jewish Research had brought in several important speakers and even though my Free Thinking Film Festival was just a week away, I couldn't pass up the opportunity.

Walking into the Chevra Kadisha Synagogue on Clanranald Avenue brought back memories of growing up on Oxford Avenue in Montreal. My old bar mitzvah teacher prayed there and he used to urge me, with very little success, to attend Shabbat services there. The last time I was inside the Shul was when my best friend growing up, Mark Satz, had his bar mitzvah there in 1969.

We walked in and sat down at a large round table in the function hall. It was like going back in time — Mark's sister had her wedding reception in this room in the mid-1960s, and I remember being allowed to drink several whiskey sours. A slightly drunk 10-year-old stumbled home when it was over.

The gentleman sitting next to me was about 85 years old and we struck up a conversation. I told him that I had just produced a documentary showing that the CBC was biased against Israel and that I was going to show it in Ottawa in a week's time.

He started to laugh.

I asked him what was so funny, and he replied in a thick Yiddish accent, "I need a documentary to tell me the CBC is biased?"

I understood his point. If you want to hear a whole auditorium laugh, just tell a crowd of Jewish people that the CBC is fair and balanced when it comes to Israel. Or tell an audience of conservatives that the CBC gives voice to their issues and concerns.

I know. I've done it.

It's not just me, and it isn't just conservatives or people who think well of Israel who regard the CBC as biased to the "left." An IPSOS/Reid poll from September 2010 I obtained under an Access to Information request shows that while Canadian consumers "envision themselves as being essentially balanced in terms of ideology," they see the CBC as ideologically well to the "left" of themselves and of almost every other media source. The survey looked at public perceptions of the CBC, BBC, Global, MSNBC, CTV, The Globe and Mail, CNN, The National Post, and Fox News. CBC was viewed as the farthest to the left, with the BBC coming in second. Not surprisingly, the National Post and Fox News were viewed as being on the right.

In the 2011 election, almost 40 per cent of the Canadian electorate voted for the Conservative Party. Now, I wouldn't expect or want the CBC to lean to the right, but I would have liked to hear some conservative voices on their public affairs shows. Sometimes, Don Cherry would come up as an example of a conservative voice, but he was just a colourful character on *Hockey Night in Canada*. His job was to entertain viewers. His trademark was his outrageously loud suits. In 2006, the CBC hired another colourful character, Kevin O'Leary, to play a hardline venture capitalist on Dragon's Den, a reality-television program. Three years later, O'Leary was hired to play the role of the "colourful, outspoken and controversial" co-host of the *Lang and O'Leary Exchange* — a hybrid business-entertainment show. Notably, the CBC ombudsman once chastised O'Leary as having violated the public broadcaster's standards by referring to a guest, the far-left Occupy Wall Street ideologue Chris Hedges, as someone who sounded like "a left-wing nutbar." O'Leary left the CBC.

One senior CBC personality who came to be known as a conservative voice is Rex Murphy, a proud Newfoundlander and host of the immensely popular *Cross Country Checkup*. On that show, Murphy was expected to be generously even-handed and to keep his views to himself. Murphy was allowed to wear his heart on his sleeve in his editorials for CBC's *The National*, however. But Murphy was the sole exception to the rule, the odd man out in the CBC's corporate culture. If you go back and check the CBC's annual Massey Lectures, you'll find any number of liberal-left luminaries. You'll find Noam Chomsky, even, but certainly not William F. Buckley.

Like many Canadians, I grew up on the CBC. It was an important part of my life, particularly when I lived in Toronto in the early 1980s. Back then I didn't have a television and so I relied upon CBC radio for everything. It was the soundtrack of my life and there was nothing better than spending a Sunday morning reading the New York Times while listening to the CBC. I was proud back then that even Americans were tuning into *As It Happens* — they thought the nightly segment of Parliamentary debate highlights was hugely entertaining. And, to me, Shelagh Rogers was the voice of Canada and could no wrong.

I never really thought about whether the CBC was biased, unfair or unbalanced. I was a man of the left and I liked what I heard.

When I came back to Canada in 2000 after my years away in the United States, Britain and Asia, the CBC I'd known and loved was gone. Of course, I had changed as well, but identity politics had crept into all the major public affairs shows and my beloved *As It Happens* was a shadow of its former self. It just didn't have the same seriousness and depth that I remembered from the early 1980s with hosts Alan Maitland, Barbara Frum and Elizabeth Gray.

After 9/11, I would listen only to get my blood boiling, and boy did it boil. *The Current*, started in 2002, was politically biased well to the left. Michael Enright on Sunday mornings was embarrassingly shallow and his distaste for Israel was palpable. *Dispatches with Rick MacInnes-Rae* was completely unserious — in 2002 one of his guests was the 9/11 Truther Michael Springmann. The local Ottawa morning show had me reaching for a shoe on a continual basis.

This was at a time when Canada was fighting in Afghanistan, the
Americans were in Iraq and much of the world was confronting the
threat of Islamist terrorism. The CBC could have been bringing us
major intellectual voices from across Canada and around the world —
but unfortunately, its rolodex was so limited and its corporate culture
so stale that it seemed impossible for CBC producers to think outside
their high-tech box on Front Street in Toronto. Canadians were exposed
to an extremely narrow range of "progressive" voices who made sense
of the post 9/11 world only in an old and faded anti-American, "anti-
imperialist," Chomskyite context. Then there was the CBC's embrace of
the radical-chic and its preoccupations with pop culture, which only
added another layer of frivolousness to CBC programming. In 2006,
Tony Burman, the CBC News Editor in Chief and the corporation's head
of English-language news and current affairs programming, explained
to the Toronto Star that in 2004 the CBC had conducted a "sweeping
survey" of 1,200 Canadians that found "parts of the operation didn't
appeal to young people." A later Star article referring to a CBC study
(perhaps it was the same study) quoted Jennifer McGuire, CBC Radio's
Executive Director of Programming: "We went into people's homes and
looked at their record collections. It was a fairly in-depth and exhaustive
piece of research." The Star noted: "Half the CBC radio audience is
over 65 and the changes are aimed at attracting younger listeners." So,
changes were necessary.

The first change was to hire Avi Lewis and George
Stroumboulopoulos.

Lewis, who'd cut his teeth as host of *The New Music*, a music
magazine show on the MuchMusic cable channel and Citytv, was a scion
of the Toronto high-society Lewis family. His grandfather was federal
NDP leader David Lewis. His father Stephen was an outspoken former
leader of the Ontario NDP and CBC broadcaster. His mother Michele
Landsberg was a colourful left-wing Toronto Star columnist. His partner
was anti-globalization activist superstar Naomi Klein. The CBC picked
up Avi Lewis to host the hip political-affairs show *Counterspin* in the late

1990s, and later he hosted the CBC public affairs shows *The Big Picture* and *On the Map*.

George Stroumboulopoulos was a rock jock from Kelowna, B.C., who had gone on to work as an entertainment reporter and producer-host of *The Punk Show* and *The New Music* program for MuchMusic. Following a brief stint serving as the "advocate" for NDP patriarch Tommy Douglas in the CBC's *Greatest Canadian* competition series, Stroumboulopoulos was elevated in 2005, straight into the job as host of *The Hour*, a CBC Newsworld current affairs television program.

"With its vertigo-inducing graphics, cheeky sensibility, quirky stories, and multi-pierced host, ex-MuchMusic vee-jay George Stroumboulopoulos, *The Hour* certainly looks like nothing else on Newsworld," The Toronto Star observed at the time. "Unlike some other CBC hipsters, past and present, 'Strombo' is the real deal." The guests on *The Hour* give a sense of the sort of show it was to become.

From the Strombo guest list I acquired through an Access to Information request: The noted "anti-imperialist" Robert Fisk (at least twice), the Reverend Jesse Jackson (twice), the Globe and Mail's former Maoist columnist Jan Wong (three times), NDP leader Jack Layton (six times), Avi Lewis's dad Stephen (eight times, including two appearances with his wife and Avi's mother, Michele Landsberg), the later-disgraced CBC hipster icon Jian Ghomeshi (10 times), the American counterculture heroes Noam Chomsky, Howard Zinn, Cindy Sheehan, Ralph Nader, Gore Vidal, Chris Hedges, Angela Davis and Jeremy Scahill, the celebrity CBC scientist and environmentalist prophet David Suzuki (seven times), failed Democratic Party presidential hopeful and anti-global warming crusader Al Gore (three times), Naomi Klein (twice), left-wing literary maven Margaret Atwood (three times), American "anti-war" documentary filmmaker Michael Moore (three times), famous American military deserter Jeremy Hinzman (twice), and the famous Canadian left-wingers Judy Rebick and Olivia Chow.

It wasn't all one-sided — the conservative journalist and former George Bush speechwriter David Frum was on several times, and several Canadian Conservative politicians appeared on the show, but these appearances seemed token efforts at balance.

Perhaps the most embarrassing show featured Strombo's March 30, 2009, conversation by video hookup with the disgraced British "anti-war" MP George Galloway, whose celebrity status in Canada had been enhanced by his supporters' claims that Ottawa had "banned" him from entering the country. Strombo never challenged Galloway's version of events, which didn't hold up against the facts. Immigration officials had merely warned him that if he were to proceed with his intention to visit Toronto for one of his many "anti-war" engagements, he might find himself turned away. A few weeks earlier, Galloway had handed a pile of cash — 25,000 British pounds — to Hamas leader Ismail Haniya. Hamas is a listed terrorist organization in Canada. In a speech from a podium in Gaza, Galloway had declared: "Here is the money, this is not charity. This is not charity, this is politics." Even a court petition by Galloway's Canadian supporters resulted in a judge concluding that there was no "ban" for him to consider, to either overturn or uphold.

A year later, Galloway was back on Strombo's show, but in person, and he denied making any political contribution to Hamas, saying the money he provided was for the Hamas "Ministry of Health" and that it was proper that the money go straight to Haniya. Stroumboulopoulos didn't even pursue questions of Galloway's claim. Strombo's tone during the entire 15-minute interview was one of fawning admiration.

Like Stroumboulopoulos, Avi Lewis came out of Citytv's MuchMusic, but Lewis had been *The New Music* show's "political specialist." Lewis's CBC debut was a new show, *Counterspin*, which he hosted from 1998 to 2001. CBC brought Lewis back in 2006 to host *The Big Picture*, an audience-participation public affairs show, and the following year he was hosting a daily public affairs program called *On the Map*, a briefly lived effort that showcased a stream of cool anti-American bias and sneering condescension. In one particularly embarrassing episode, Lewis confronted the renowned Muslim dissident Ayaan Hirsi Ali. Ali laughed at him.

Lewis was aghast that Ali had dismissed his assertions that North American Muslims felt "under siege" and were afraid to contribute to charities or travel by air because they'd "end up on a list somewhere" or find themselves "in detention for years without ever seeing charges against them." Ali had said Lewis was exaggerating and that the United States was "the best democracy."

Lewis: *Is there a school where they teach you these American clichés? Is it part of your application process? I'm so upset that I am losing my guard here. I can't believe you just said that.*

Ali: *You grew up in freedom and so you can spit at freedom because you don't know what is like not to have freedom. I haven't. I know there is many things wrong in America and I know that there any many things wrong with Americans, but I still believe it's the best nation in the world.*

For a "counter-narrative" to the situation in Gaza, Lewis turned to former British Intelligence officer Alastair Crooke for a segment called "Debunking Gaza's Civil War." Crooke's organization, Conflicts Forum, argues that the West should politically engage with Hamas and other radical Islamists. On Lewis's show, Crooke argued that Hamas would bring law and order and tranquillity to daily life in Gaza, if left undisturbed. Lewis was impressed. In a show on women In Afghanistan, Lewis relied on Ann Jones, a regular contributor to The Nation Magazine, who touted the views of the former Afghan MP Malalai Joya, a minor and nearly forgotten figure in Afghanistan but a fixture in western "anti-war" circles. Joya had stood beside Jack Layton at the NDP's 2006 "troops out" convention in Quebec.

Another young hipster the CBC hired was Jian Ghomeshi, the former drummer-singer of the popular rock band Moxy Früvous. Ghomeshi was taken on as the showcase host of a new and cool art, culture and entertainment magazine program called simply Q. An enormous amount of resources were poured into Q, and while it would have been fine enough if it had kept to interviews with rock stars and entertainment personalities, the show doubled down on the formula at work with Strombo and Lewis, to similarly annoying result.

Ghomeshi and Q provided the same welcoming platform to the same counter-culture, left-wing and radical-chic celebrities from the Strombo rolodex: Angela Davis, Michael Moore, Al Gore, David Suzuki, Ralph Nader, Naomi Klein and Olivia Chow. Along with these, Ghomeshi hosted Avi Lewis, Wikileaks founder and rape-charge fugitive Julian Assange, celebrity state-secret paranoid Glenn Greenwald, NDP strategist Brad Lavigne, *Vagina Monologues* playwright Eve Ensler, and feminist conspiracy-theorist Naomi Wolf. As a bonus, Ghomeshi occasionally threw in political commentary from the likes of Canadian rock legend Neil Young and earnest children's troubadour Raffi.

When not projecting his own political views through his guest list, Ghomeshi would occasionally show his hand. Ayaan Hirsi Ali, who had inadvertently embarrassed Avi Lewis, was a guest on Q in June 2010. Ghomeshi seemed most interested in why she had ended up with the American Enterprise Institute, a conservative think tank. Ali explained that she should be evaluated on the merit of her own arguments. She also challenged Ghomeshi on the presumption that her viewpoints on women in the Muslim world were in any way right-wing.

When Michael Moore was a guest on Q on Sept. 21, 2011, Ghomeshi introduced him by playing his famous speech at the Oscars when he berated George Bush. After the clip, Ghomeshi sighs, "Wow! I still get chills hearing that." The day before Remembrance Day 2011, Ghomeshi hosted British "anti-war" journalist Robert Fisk, who had also appeared on Strombo's show, to explain why Canadians should not wear poppies. Ghomeshi's weekly media panel usually featured Jonathan Kay, John Cruikshank and Judy Rebick. Kay was the Editorial Page Editor of the National Post at the time, the CBC's image of a hip conservative they could live with — good-looking, suave and interested in video games and the latest electronic gadgets. Cruikshank took up the centre ground. Rebick to represent the "left," was the co-founder of the Toronto webzine Rabble, the postmodernist platform that had taken off after 9/11 (a judge in a libel case would go on to characterize Rabble as the left-wing version of Free Dominion, a far-right internet discussion forum).

These were the ways the CBC tried to draw in younger listeners of a CBC-type disposition, and for a time it worked. At its zenith, Strombo's *The Hour* and Ghomeshi's *Q* were enormously popular among the under-65 crowd. For a while, *Q* was the CBC's highest-rated show in its mid-morning time slot, ever.

Ultimately, the experiment failed. Ghomeshi left the CBC under a black cloud as a notorious "bad date" and the accused in trials involving six women and several charges of sexual assault. Like a Soviet institution airbrushing its history, the CBC had its staff remove Ghomeshi murals from the walls at head office and busied itself expunging its web archives of his presence. Stroumboulopoulos was exiled to *Hockey Night in Canada*. Avi Lewis, whose show mysteriously disappeared in 2007, showed up shortly thereafter at Al Jazeera, the Qatari news organization richly funded by Qatar's ruling emir, where he devoted his talents to criticizing western-style democracy.

But the unserious and sometimes toxic political culture behind the Strombo-Lewis-Ghomeshi effort did not begin or end with them, and was not confined to the CBC's opinion or entertainment features. It would often show up in what CBC News presented as serious analysis, most noticeably in the years immediately following 9/11, when the head of the CBC's English-language services and current affairs programming was Tony Burman.

Burman was the CBC honcho who had ended up involved in the 2003 controversy about the CBC's aversion to the term "terrorist." Like Avi Lewis, Burman would join the Qatari-owned Al Jazeera after his 35-year run with the CBC ended in 2007, around the same time Lewis joined Al Jazeera. Burman was picked up as managing director of Al Jazeera English. In 2010, he became Al Jazeera's chief strategic advisor for the Americas.

The corporate culture that had provided such easy career paths for Berman, Lewis, Stroumboulopoulos and Ghomeshi was reflected clearly in the CBC News network's standards for news analysis. These skewed standards carried on long after Burman's departure, most noticeably in CBC News analysis of American foreign policy and of events in the Middle East, Afghanistan and Israel. You could see it at work in the expert commentary the corporation provided its viewers and listeners. Two instructive cases in point involve the CBC's reliance on the "experts" Michael Scheuer and Eric Margolis.

Data from a 2014 Access to Information request I completed indicates that Michael Scheuer appeared on CBC shows a total of 35 times between 2004 and 2013, including eight appearances on *The National* and five appearances on *Power & Politics*. In addition, many segments of his interviews were repeated on local shows across the country (he was still showing up on CBC broadcasts when I was writing this book). As for Eric Margolis, he would sometimes be introduced as "our foreign affairs analyst" or "the CBC's Eric Margolis" or simply Eric Margolis, "reporting for the CBC." It's hard to say just how routinely or how often Margolis has appeared in CBC broadcasts. In 2014, the CBC was calling Margolis "a regular contributor" to CBC News, but for some reason my Access to Information request for the number of his appearances on the network was refused by CBC management (at the time of writing this book, the ruling was under appeal).

So, who are Michael Scheuer and Eric Margolis?

The CBC typically presented Scheuer as a former CIA analyst, operative or special adviser, and occasionally as the author of the 2004 book, *Imperial Hubris*. You'd never know it from watching CBC News, but Scheuer, who worked on the CIA's Osama bin Laden desk prior to 9/11 — not exactly a testament to his intelligence-gathering skills — was better known in the United States as a notorious far-right extremist whose views were indistinguishable from those of the loony far-left. After Scheuer came to prominence in 2004 when he was outed as the anonymous CIA analyst who had authored *Imperial Hubris*, his "expertise" and credentials were routinely employed to conveniently prop up the fashionable and dominant "anti-war" polemic in Canada.

In an interview on CBC News in January 2005, Scheuer said that "on Israel, no one, certainly not myself is suggesting abandoning the Israelis." By October 2013, Scheuer was telling a U.S. House committee that if it were up to him, "I'd dump Israel tomorrow." But this was not a case of some dramatic conversion of an apparently sober news analyst to the extremes of a far-right ideology.

Scheuer was still appearing as a respectable expert on CBC's *Power and Politics* long after he had endorsed the assassination of U.S. President Barack Obama and British Prime Minister David Cameron. He did so by favorably recalling the 17th-century English Republican Algernon Sidney's admonition that "every man might kill a tyrant, and no names are recorded in history with more honor than of those who did it."

As far back as 2004, Scheuer was calling Osama bin Laden "the most respected, loved, romantic, charismatic, and perhaps able figure in the last 150 years of Islamic history." Scheuer's "viable" foreign-policy alternative to the challenge of Al-Qaida included "the elimination of the Jewish state" and its replacement with "an Islamic Palestinian state" and "the replacement of U.S.-protected Muslim regimes that do not govern according to Islam by regimes that do." In 2005, he told Al Jazeera that "criticizing Israel in the United States is like a martyrdom operation." In his 2008 book *Marching Towards Hell*, Scheuer calls both the U.S. Democratic Party and the Republican Party "wholly owned subsidiaries of the American Israeli Public Affairs Committee (AIPAC)."

As for Eric Margolis, the expert the CBC often called "our foreign affairs analyst" or "the CBC's Eric Margolis" or the CBC's "regular contributor," his credentials may be a bit questionable, but the CBC's reluctance to disclose just how heavily the network relied on him was downright mysterious.

In 2012, CBC News Executive Editor Esther Enkin, in the course of answering a complaint that Margolis was not a credible expert and was inordinately hostile to Israel, called Margolis a regular CBC contributor of several years' standing who was "widely viewed as a foreign affairs expert, especially in matters concerning the Middle East." The complaint was triggered by a segment that featured Margolis analyzing the 2011 elections in Egypt. CBC Ombudsman Kirk Lapointe weighed in, saying that it was fair to call Margolis a foreign affairs analyst and it was "not necessary to review his background." The CBC's error was to present him as a correspondent of some kind, although Margolis "certainly had the credentials to appear as a credible guest," Lapointe wrote, because he had witnessed events in Egypt firsthand.

So, just who was Eric Margolis? Was he really a foreign affairs expert?

Until 2014, Margolis was the longtime owner and chairman of Jamieson Laboratories, Canada's largest manufacturer of vitamins and supplements. He is an expert, of sorts. He is the author of two books — *American Raj*, which is more or less a condemnation of American imperialism in the so-called Muslim World, and *War at the Top of the World*, which covers much of the same ground but in Central Asia. From his swish Forest Hills mansion in Toronto, Margolis wrote a column for the conservative Sun newspaper chain for nearly 30 years (the chain dumped him unceremoniously in 2010), and also regularly supplied analysis to the far-right webzine LewRockwell.com.

Perhaps best known for its conspiracy theories about AIDs and the JFK assassination, LewRockwell.com also regularly published contributors such as Michael Scheuer and 9/11 truther Paul Craig Roberts. Margolis dabbled in 9/11 conspiracy theory himself. A decade after the Sept. 11 attacks, Margolis was still insisting there was no evidence implicating Osama bin Laden in the atrocity. In 2004, Margolis accused Israel of assassinating PLO chairman Yasser Arafat with poison. Deeply sympathetic to the Pakistani establishment and hostile to Afghan forces opposing the Taliban, Margolis was a key contributor to the far-right Republican Pat Buchanan's American Conservative magazine.

While I was working on this book, as far as I could tell his last appearance on CBC News was on July 27, 2014, during the Hamas-Israel war — according to Margolis, it was all Israeli Prime Minister Benjamin Netanyahu's fault, of course.

Prior to 9/11, Margolis was a respectable journalist who freelanced for a variety of reputable newspapers. Curiously, even while the CBC was claiming him as "our foreign affairs analyst" or "the CBC's Eric Margolis," he sometimes appeared on other television networks, like CTV and Ontario's TVO. But after 9/11, just like Scheuer, Margolis was a right-wing crank who could be reliably depended upon to provide the CBC with "analysis" that dovetailed nicely with even the crazier "anti-imperialist" crowd within the liberal-left demographic that the CBC catered to.

By 9/11, all of CBC's news and current affairs programming was in the hands of Tony Burman, the senior CBC executive who would go on to work for Al Jazeera. By March 2002, Burman was the editor in chief of CBC's English-language services. By 2011 he'd left Al Jazeera and returned to Canada to teach journalism at Ryerson University in Toronto and to write columns for the Toronto Star.

Some of Burman's column headlines: "Charlie Hebdo — The case for not reprinting;" "Iran steps up, leaving Canada, Israel alone;" "Time for Canada, Israel to stop living in a fantasy world;" "Iran's critics, full of sound and fury;" "America ripe for a new revolution;" "Peace in Syria requires Iran, not bombing;" "Canadian extremism — we're wrong on Iran;" "Invading Iran: why resistance is now crucial;" "Ottawa unwise to echo Netanyahu." On Jan. 21, 2012, he predicted: "There will be a war in the Middle East within the next several months, triggered by an Israeli attack on Iran." In Sept. 7, 2012, after Canada closed the Iranian Embassy in Ottawa, he called Benjamin Netanyahu Canada's "new foreign minister," and accused Stephen Harper's government of "outsourcing" Canada's Middle East policy to Jerusalem.

That should give you an idea of the tenor of CBC's news and current affairs broadcasting in the years following 9/11.

For a short period during the Burman years, there was some oversight, sharp criticism and even some public debate about the CBC. During 2003 and 2004, the National Post ran a regular column, CBC Watch, which documented the public corporation's left-wing bias. But monitoring the CBC's excesses was a job that fell mainly to

HonestReporting Canada, an NGO with a focus on the news media's anti-Israel bias. From its founding in 2003, HonestReporting went on to file about 1,000 complaints to the CBC over the following decade. About 70 per cent of its complaints were sustained to HonestReporting's satisfaction.

After launching in 2011, the Sun News Network filed hundreds of Access to Information requests with the CBC. The loud, conservative gadfly of Canadian journalism fought running battles with the CBC's gatekeepers, sometimes scoring news from the effort. One Sun story exposed the $1 million cost of an opera based on the life of Brian Mulroney that was never broadcast. In another scoop, a Sun News reporter found that CBC Hubert Lacroix had been forced to reimburse the corporation for roughly $30,000 in dodgy travel expenses. Sun News could be over the top, but its crusade against the publicly funded CBC hit a nerve. So I decided that the Free Thinking Film Society should produce our own documentary on the CBC.

Examining the structural, cultural and institutional biases of the CBC would be a daunting challenge. The CBC is a huge organization with almost $2 billion in revenues (roughly 60 per cent coming from the federal treasury) and about 7,000 employees providing radio, television and online services in the two official languages as well as eight aboriginal languages. We could have easily made our film about a host of problems at the CBC — it's Toronto-centricity, its anti-Americanism, its obsession with identity politics, its cultural insularity, and so on and so forth. We decided to focus on the CBC's bias against Israel and its bias against small 'c' and large 'C' conservatives. But it was the CBC's antipathy to Israel that was most egregious.

I contacted Mike Fegelman of HonestReporting Canada and he sent me a USB stick with 120 clips from a variety of CBC shows. We spent hours searching YouTube, and several bloggers sent us ideas and video. We spent the whole summer watching, downloading and editing videos, adding titles and subtitles and writing commentary. By the time fall had arrived, we had produced a 50-minute documentary, *This Hour*

Could Have 10,000 Minutes: The Biases of the CBC.

What we showed was that Israel would sometimes get dragged into stories that had nothing to do with Israel, that the CBC would run puff pieces in place of serious reports on such stories as the Canadian boat to Gaza, and reports would sometimes include interviews with 9/11 Truthers and other anti-Israel cranks. The CBC's anti-Conservative bias would sometimes sneak into weather reports, and even game shows could turn political. Comedy shows often embedded anti-Conservative bias in completely unfunny skits. The CBC even managed to turn Obama's visit to Canada into a story mocking Stephen Harper. But it was on the subject of Israel that the CBC routinely failed to demonstrate even the slightest degree of journalistic objectivity. Radio-Canada was the worst.

Just one example of Radio-Canada's bias was an April 9, 2010, program titled *Canada and the Lobby: How the Pro-Israel Lobby is changing Canadian policy towards the Middle-East.* The documentary presented the Conservative government's efforts to reign in the federally funded agency Rights & Democracy as a case of "acquiescing" to the Israel lobby, of a piece with federal cuts to NGOs that supported Israel Apartheid Week and court challenges to Israeli policies. The documentary disputed the view that the UN Relief Works Agency's textbooks were anti-Israel and claimed that the Canadian government had made a mistake in cutting UNRWA funding.

The former Canadian diplomat Robert Fowler is shown claiming that "the scramble to lock up the Jewish vote in Canada meant selling out our widely admired and long-established reputation for fairness and justice in this most volatile and dangerous region in the world." The show's host, Luc Chartrand, says "the Jewish lobby, the Israel lobby" is doing nothing illegal, and is not "a clandestine operation," but "we see deep down a will to equate criticism of Israel with anti-Semitism, a will to punish groups that criticize Israel by cutting off their funds and to see the government for part and parcel of this operation, a certain witch-hunt."

There was so much evidence of the CBC's bias against Israel, making our documentary was less an effort in gathering the evidence than in deciding how much to leave out.

From July to August 2009, the CBC Radio's popular *As It Happens* program aired three shows with segments on Israeli "war crimes" allegedly committed during Israel's three-week Gaza incursion that had concluded in January that year. On July 1, Mark Garlasco of Human Rights Watch alleged that Israel had deliberately targeted and killed Palestinian civilians including children. On August 13, *As It Happens* presented an interview with Joe Stork of Human Rights Watch, who made similar allegations. On Sept. 17, *As It Happens* interviewed Judge Richard Goldstone, the head of a U.N. fact-finding mission that had produced a hotly disputed report on the Gaza conflict. Goldstone told the CBC that "war crimes" were committed on both sides, but he mostly spoke about Israel.

In all three shows, the Israeli government's side of the story was absent. This prompted a complaint to the CBC from Paul Michaels, Director of Communications for the Canada-Israel Committee, but *As It Happens* producer Lynda Shorten replied that it was "not incumbent to balance within a single program, but that balance could be achieved over time." The CBC ombudsman concurred, but added: "I think it fair to say that on a subject fraught with controversy as this, most listeners would have found it appropriate to hear a reflection of Israel's position sometime in the aftermath of the report's release." The ombudsman ruled that the *As It Happens* report on Goldstone's findings was a clear violation of the CBC's policies on fairness and balance.

But the CBC's policies on fairness and balance were, to say the least, malleable.

On Jan. 27, 2011, *Power & Politics* hosted a discussion between Clifford May, President of the Foundation for Defense of Democracies, and Thomas Woodley, President of Canadians for Justice and Peace in the Middle East (CJPME). Woodley asserted that democracy existed in Gaza. May strongly disagreed that Hamas was democratic. In a letter to a complainant who claimed that the CJPME was an anti-Israel hate group, CBC News executive editor Esther Enkin wrote that CBC's mandate under the Broadcasting Act required the network to present differing points of view on controversial subjects, but the CBC was not obliged to determine what the truth was — or what views were "acceptable." The CBC required only "to present differing views fairly and accurately affording Canadians the opportunity and the information they need to make up their own minds about the nature or the quality of the views expressed."

In response to a complaint about a report on *The National* on Aug. 27, 2008, that alluded to Israel having not forgotten that Iranian president Mahmoud Ahmadinejad had at the very least implied a disturbing threat against Israel, "to wipe it off the map," Esther Enkin wrote that some controversy had surrounded the statement's translation. Consequently, the threat should be presented as such by "those who believe that is what he meant." The CBC Ombudsman agreed that "it would have been more accurate" to present Ahmadinejad's remark in that way. But there were some at the CBC who clearly felt that Iran was not a threat to Israel, but rather that Israel was perhaps a threat to Iran.

On Nov. 21, 2011, after the International Atomic Energy Agency released a damning report on Iran's quest to procure nuclear weapons, *As It Happens'* Carol Off interviewed Chris Alexander, Parliamentary Secretary to the Minister of Defense. "Given that Iran is next to a nuclear power — that is Israel — is there any way you can look at Iran's possible development of nuclear weapons as a defensive act," Off asked Alexander, "and not an act of provocation?" Alexander kept referring back to the IAEA report, but Off wouldn't give it up. "Is it legal for Israel to have nuclear weapons?"

CBC again cast Iran as being in need of protection from Israel in a documentary by Alexandre Trudeau, former Liberal Prime Minister Pierre Trudeau's son and soon-to-be Liberal leader Justin Trudeau's brother. The documentary, *The New Great Game*, appeared on *The National* on Oct. 14, 2012. The film was produced in cooperation with Press TV, the Iranian state-owned broadcaster. At one point, the documentary narrator asserts: "While there is no proof that Iran has even made the decision to start a nuclear arms program, Israel's nuclear arsenal will largely outgun whatever weapons Iran might acquire. But from the vantage point of Iran, it is the one being threatened, not the one doing the threatening." The film then turns to Noam Chomsky who asks: "What country in the world could have a greater need for deterrent?" And then the narrator: "Lacking the ultimate deterrent in nuclear weapons, Iran only has conventional forces to defend itself from an attack."

Sometimes the CBC's attitude problem just made you laugh.

In January of 2014, the Canadian government appointed Vivian Bercovici as the new ambassador to Israel. Evan Solomon, host of *Power & Politics,* had Foreign Affairs Minister John Baird as his guest to discuss the appointment. Here is the exchange:

Solomon: Why not appoint someone from the diplomatic corps? Obviously this is a very sensitive position. I mean Vivian Bercovici is Jewish, so there are going to be some questions. Why not appoint someone who doesn't even have the perception of any kind of bias?

Baird: Well, Evan, I didn't ask what religion she was. I didn't ask what...

Solomon: But you must have done your research. I mean, to be fair, is that disingenuous?

Baird: Her name looks Italian. No, in fact, before offering the position, I did not know she was Jewish. That's not the way our government runs things. We look for people who are talented and capable and can do the job, regardless of what religious background they have. In Canada, Evan, it's actually illegal for employers to do just that. She has a unique amount of experience, as a lawyer, someone who has lived in the area, someone who knows the file and someone who will advance Canada's interests.

Not surprisingly, the issues of Islam, Islamism and terrorism tended to befuddle the CBC. In Ottawa, the CBC assigned reporter Lucy van Oldenbarneveld to cover these issues locally. Her reporting could stand as a case study of the CBC's corporate-culture befuddlement.

A June 10, 2010, interview Oldenbarneveld conducted with Ayaan Hirsi Ali in Ottawa was like a combined replication of Ali's encounters with Jian Ghomeshi and Avi Lewis. Oldenbarneveld asked what Ali said to people who accused her "of just allowing the white liberal masses to be comfortable with their own prejudices." Ali answered that it was rather Islam's apologists who insist that Islam is not violent who provide "white liberals" with an excuse to ignore human rights violations committed in the name of Islam.

In October 2010, Tarek Fatah launched his new book, *The Jew is Not My Enemy*, at the Ottawa Writers Festival, in a discussion format with Oldenbarneveld. Fatah was funny, serious and resolute in his defense of western values. Fatah said that because he was left of centre and a former member of the New Democratic Party, he was particularly dismayed by the betrayal of enlightenment values by people like Jack Layton, who was NDP leader at the time. Fatah's book was about Muslim anti-Semitism, but Oldenbarneveld's first five questions were either about Islamophobia or the burqa. Oldenbarneveld's final question of the day turned back to the burqa, and whether women in Canada who wore burqas were admirably independent for doing so.

Oldenbarneveld repeated her performance on Sept. 21, 2011, when she hosted a book launch for Irshad Manji's *Allah, Liberty & Love*. Oldenbarneveld wanted Manji to talk about whether "Muslims feel under siege" a decade after 9/11, whether Muslim women who wear the hijab "feel attacked and criticized and scrutinized," and whether "non-Muslims can approach a conversation like that with no judgement." Manji demurred, saying that nobody approaches questions like that without judgement: "Can you please, Lucy, apply standards, universal standards, to both Muslims and non-Muslims? Can you nudge yourself to do that? I'd really appreciate that because that is the essence of good journalism." She added: "Please do not treat Muslims like children."

Further evidence that the CBC was just not up to the job when it came to Islamist terrorism was the attack on Charlie Hebdo in France in January 2015. David Studer, Director, Journalism Standards and Practices at CBC News, wrote that "we aren't showing cartoons making fun of the Prophet Muhammad. Other elements of Charlie Hebdo's content and style are fine, but his area should be avoided as, quite simply, it's offensive to Muslims as a group." Talk about bigotry — here was the CBC lumping all Muslims into a single group.

Even by 2011, there was no way I could fit all the material I'd gathered about the CBC's biases into the Free Thinking Film documentary I was putting together. Unsurprisingly, when it came out, it didn't make me any friends at the CBC. I'd tried to get the CBC involved in a debate about the film's merits and made an effort to promote the film at the CBC's Annual Meeting in early November 2011 at the War Museum. I asked the CBC's CEO, Hubert Lacroix, if he would send someone to sit on the CBC panel at our upcoming film festival. Lacroix said no, because my festival was just an "opportunity for people of like-minds to have a conversation amongst themselves."

He knew about my film. I had emailed more than 60 CBC producers and hosts asking for somebody to participate in the panel discussion following the film. I'd also personally invited several local CBC hosts to attend. I also sent email invitations to every member of the CBC's Board of Directors, offering them copies of my film. Only one board member took me up on my offer. He later told me he agreed with the premise of my documentary — it was a private correspondence so it would be wrong to say who it was.

In 2012, I filed an Access to Information Request to get all the internal communications about my documentary. There was clearly no discussion anywhere within the CBC about the substance of my documentary, but there were many widely circulated emails between a variety of managers about my request for a panelist. One particular email contained the message "here's what we'll send," but it was followed by two redacted pages, withheld under sections of 21 (1) and 21 (1) b of the Access to Information Act, which refers to "advice or recommendations developed by or for a government institution or a minister of the Crown" and "an account of consultations or deliberations involving officers or employees of a government institution, a minister of the Crown or the staff of a minister of the Crown."

I'd never had much luck getting the CBC to cover the Free Thinking Film events, festivals or speakers, but it was even harder to get the CBC's attention after my documentary came out.

In 2012, I landed the Canadian premiere of a new film, *Death by China*, based on the book by Peter Navarro and Greg Autry. The film documents the perverted capitalism on offer by the Communist Party in China and shows how its nationalistic frenzy was becoming a threat to peace. I also arranged for Greg Autry to attend the showing so that he could answer questions about the film. It was immediately topical. There was a debate raging in Canada about China's planned takeover of the Calgary-based Nexen company by China's state-owned CNOOC, and about Canada's proposed adoption of a Foreign Investment Promotion and Protection Agreement with China.

In response to a press release I'd circulated about the film, a local CBC morning show got in touch with me and asked if Autry would be available for an interview. Because this was a last-minute request, I had to track Autry down to get him to call the CBC producers from Chicago on his way to Ottawa. Once they figured out that Autry was very cynical about China and wanted to talk about the ethics of the FIPA agreement, they proposed to balance out the interview on air with a pro-China business consultant. Autry agreed to the proposed discussion. But it was not to happen.

As Autry later explained on his website: "Shortly after, I got another call and a saccharine email, pronouncing that my ethical angle would be 'matching apples and oranges' with the business consultant that had been added to my originally scheduled interview and therefore (in the interest of 'balance.' I presume) my anti-China perspective was being dropped. Essentially, it seems, the CBC wanted a conversation full of facts and figures without a complicating discussion of human rights, the environment, and the legitimacy of the government on the other end of the deal."

So, again, I was shut out of the CBC. Maybe it was the biases embedded within the CBC's corporate culture at work again. It wasn't the first time something like this had happened. In 2007, the CBC pulled a documentary, *Beyond the Red Wall: The Persecution of the Falun Gong*, after complaints from the Chinese Embassy.

Still, nothing compares to the CBC's treatment of the Israeli-Palestinian issue. The CBC's English-language coverage was bad, but Radio-Canada was far worse. In 2007, the Radio-Canada ombudsman's annual report was downright defensive, stating that "those complaining about coverage of the Israeli-Palestinian conflict most often claim that the news has a pro-Palestinian slant. Clearly, a pro-Israel lobby is active." As if a "pro-Israel lobby" was the problem, and as if the legitimacy of a complaint could be determined by whether a complainant was pro-Israel or anti-Israel.

By 2013, after many battles, the ombudsman recognized that an attitude problem had indeed skewed Radio-Canada's coverage. The annual report for 2013 recognized that there were "again this year very real problems with the coverage of the Israeli-Palestinian conflict." There was the nuisance of the "lobby" again: "That said, we cannot pretend that the work of journalists at Radio-Canada, whether radio, television or the web, was not scrutinized by a very well-organized lobby which was as determined as it was effective." But, this time around: "This attention has had the merit of at least identifying the elements of the coverage which the management of news and information needs to improve. . . . there need to be more, perhaps changing their attitude towards the Israeli-Palestinian conflict."

The ombudsman's office had its own attitude problem, as was obvious when Pierre Tourangeau, Ombudsman for the French Services, testified before a Senate Committee in September 2014. Referring to a meeting with the director of the Centre of Israel and Jewish Affairs (CIJA) about Radio-Canada coverage, Tourangeau said: "I told him his organization was constantly attacking us and asked whether this approach may not essentially be a bit counterproductive." Nevertheless, Tourangeau conceded CIJA "was in fact often right."

There are obviously greater deficiencies in the CBC's corporate culture than the attitude problems underlying the network's biases against Israel. So, what on earth is to be done?

In November 2014, Steven Guiton, Vice President of Technology and Chief Regulatory Officer at the CBC, delivered an extensive presentation to the CBC's Board of Directors, which was shared in early 2015 with the Standing Senate Committee on Transport and Communications. What was apparent from Guiton's overview was that the CBC was not at all sure what to do in an environment where everything is in flux.

With revenues of $1.9 billion, of which 60 per cent comes from government, the CBC and Radio-Canada maintains more than 100 stations (88 radio and 27 TV). But specialty TV is the fastest growing broadcast category. Internet advertising now exceeds all television advertising. Residential TV subscriber numbers are in decline. A huge fragmentation of audiences is under way. Of the top 100 TV programs in Canada by 2014, only 23 were Canadian-produced and one-third of Anglophone Canadians had embraced Netflix.

Coping with the changing environment was tough enough, but part of the problem was that the Harper Government had refused to set any direction for the CBC. Yes, he'd cut their budget, but his government seemed unable or unwilling to set any strategic directions for the broadcaster. This was a huge dereliction of duty and there was absolutely no excuse for it. It was unconscionable to let the CBC just hang there and try to figure things out on its own.

The Broadcasting Act of 1991 mandates its two "primary tools," the CBC and the Canadian Radio-Television and Telecommunications Commission. Section 3 of the Act covers the CBC, and part of its mandate is to "reflect Canada and its regions to national and regional audiences, while serving the special needs of those regions."

That is where the CBC is losing sight of its mission. The ivory tower on Front Street in Toronto not only makes the CBC Toronto-centric, but it blinds them to the needs and requirements of people across the country. I remember watching the CBC News Network when what Canadians were thinking about a particular issue was presented by having a small crew go downstairs to interview people on Front Street. We've all heard these kinds of complaints. The former mayor of Iqaluit once told me the CBC was just Torontonians telling northerners how to live their lives. Herb Davis, former host of the most popular TV show in Newfoundland, *Land & Sea*, told me that he once received a memo from the Toronto head office saying they were moving his program in order to show *Mary Tyler Moore*. Entire regions of Canada seem to feel disconnected from the CBC. You've got many conservatives and many Jewish people who feel the CBC is actually hostile to their views.

You've got a CBC that continues to hit well below its weight. In February 2015, the CBC website ran a story that the headline sums up accurately: "Justin Trudeau 'thrills' Liberal crowd in Thunder Bay, Ont. *'My heart is still racing,' supporter Gloria Gabrijelcic says after meeting Liberal leader.*" Do these kind of stories help explain why the Postmedia websites gets 10 per cent more visitors per month than CBC.ca?

The "sweeping" 2004 survey that the CBC conducted of its audience resulted in a lesson, according to the Toronto Star, that "Canadians want high-quality information, more original journalism and more in-depth investigative coverage." Instead, for some reason, CBC management gave us Strombo, Ghomeshi and Lewis.

At the 2011 CBC annual meeting I attended, CBC president Hubert Lacroix said his mission was to reach more Canadians, with more transmitters, and to extend the CBC's reach throughout every part of the country. A laudable goal, for sure.

But, he had yet to internalize the fact that the CBC had already lost large segments of the Canadian population that it could already easily reach.

Eight

My Dinner with David

It was one of those cold January nights in Ottawa. My new friend, the poet and essayist David Solway, had invited Andrew and me to dinner with his girlfriend Janice Fiamengo, an English professor at the University of Ottawa, at Janice's place in the Byward Market neighbourhood. Andrew and I were lucky to find a parking spot just across the street from Janice's place. Once inside, we were pleasantly surprised to see that Janice had made pizza, and we sat down to what should have been a delightful dinner.

Little did I know that my dinner with David would mark the beginning of my confrontation with the self-styled "counter-jihad" movement, a poisonous far-right subculture that mobilized around ideas every bit as unhinged and venomous as the "left-wing" ideas I'd recoiled from in the aftermath of 9/11.

I'd met David two years before in Montreal in 2011. He'd come out to hear Hege Storhaug, a Norwegian author and women's rights activist whom I'd brought to Canada to speak on the effects of Muslim immigration in Europe. Storhaug had just written a controversial book, *But the Greatest of These is Freedom: The Consequences of Immigration in Europe*, which deals mostly with the rapid emergence of hard-to-integrate Muslim immigrant enclaves in Norway.

Not surprisingly, topics that touched on Islam had ended up a big focus of the Free Thinking Film Society. The entire Muslim world seemed to be in an uproar. The Arab Spring was under way. There was the Danish cartoon eruption, Hamas terror rockets were being constantly fired at Israel, the Khomeinists had flattened the Green Movement in Iran and were creating havoc in Iraq, and Pakistan was imploding. Theocratic and genocidal groups like Hezbollah, the Taliban, Boko Haram and Al-Qaida continued to terrorize millions.

After the films *Iranium* and *Obsession* that had kicked off the Free Thinking Film Society and had become cause célèbres, I'd brought in speakers like Bruce Bawer and Bat Yeʾor to discuss the impact of arch-conservative Muslim values and the influence of Middle Eastern powers on European politics. I was even part of a team that brought controversial Dutch politician Geert Wilders to Ottawa. Hege Storhaug had been a good fit, and her talk in Montreal went well.

David had joined a group of us for coffee after Storhaug's talk, and I was impressed. He was a well-known and highly regarded Montreal poet, maybe a bit intimidating, but we had mutual friends and we'd hit it off. David had gone through his own political transformation, a bit like my own. On Sept. 11, 2001, he'd found himself stuck on a Greek Island. He went on to write *The Big Lie: On Terror, Antisemitism, and Identity* — partly an account of his departure from the Chomskyite left, partly an indictment of left-wing anti-Semitism and anti-Zionism, and partly a look at similarly toxic currents in the Muslim world. We seemed to have a lot in common. David had ended up a fixture on American conservative webzines like PJ Media and FrontPage Magazine.

David was a dense but brilliant writer and had a wonderful way with words, although he clearly held some pretty eccentric political views. We began calling each other on a semi-regular basis, and I eventually helped him launch two of his books through the Free Thinking Film Society. He was spending more time in Ottawa visiting Janice, so we'd been seeing each other quite a bit.

When Andrew and I joined him and Janice for dinner that cold January night in 2013, I had no clue that before the evening was over, our friendship would be ruptured. The counter-jihad movement had everything to do with it.

It's not that I was unaware that a lot of crazy ideas were infecting public debates about Islamist terror. Sometimes I'd notice unpleasant murmurings at the margins of Free Thinking Film Society events, and there was a lot of plain nastiness in the way people talked about the fanaticism that seemed to be pouring out of Islam. I'd personally encountered some pretty unsettling attitudes in Washington, D.C., at a 2009 free-speech gathering that focused on religious issues. At Free Thinking Film events, I'd occasionally notice those attitudes among members of the Conservative Party. I'd chalked up most of this to people who just weren't very smart talking about things they didn't really understand.

But, as I would discover, the counter-jihad movement enjoyed a great deal of support among conservatives, it was a dangerously toxic thing, and its activists were not just frightened people who weren't very bright. Even so, I was still surprised to discover over dinner that night that the intellectual David Solway, who had apparently studied Islam quite closely and had read several translations of the Koran, was capable of quite nasty attitudes, too.

A month before my dinner with David I'd come across a book review by Clifford May, president of the Foundation for Defense of Democracies, in the conservative American journal *National Review*. The book May reviewed was *Islamism and Islam* by the Muslim scholar Bassam Tibi, the Koret Foundation Senior Fellow at Stanford University, formerly a visiting professor at the Yale Initiative for the Interdisciplinary Study of anti-Semitism. I greatly admired Clifford May, and he strongly recommended Tibi's book. "The debate Tibi is attempting to initiate is necessary — and long overdue," May wrote.

What Tibi had set out to explain in his book is that a necessary distinction had to be drawn between Islam as a religion and the political, fundamentalist ideology of Islamism. May's review would go on to set off quite a debate all by itself among conservatives. I immediately ordered Tibi's book. I devoured it as soon as it arrived.

Tibi clarified a great deal about what I had come to suspect about the debates conservatives were having about Islam. His book exposed why the anti-Islam right, particularly the counter-jihad movement, was dangerously wrong in several ways. It was wrong to conflate Islamist extremism with Muslims generally — that much was obvious. What was not so obvious to many conservatives was just how dangerously wrong it was to conflate Islamism with Islam and to characterize Islam in its entirety as the problem.

In *Islamism and Islam*, Tibi writes: "The religious faith of Islam is not an obstacle to peace or a threat to the non-Muslim other. Islamism, on the other hand, creates deep civilizational rifts between Muslims and non-Muslims. It not only labels 'Jews and crusaders' as the enemy but also targets other non-Muslims: Hindus in Kashmir and Malaysia, Buddhists and Confucians in China and Southeast Asia, people of African animist religions in Sudan. Islamism classifies all non-Muslim people as kuffar — infidels — and thus 'enemies' of Islam. Liberal Muslims are not immune, either."

Because David had become so preoccupied with the subject of Islam, anti-Semitism and the decline of the United States, I figured he'd be interested in Tibi's book. I brought my copy to dinner to lend him. I told him I thought it was a great book and that he might like to read it. The whole dinner turned south from there, and in a hurry.

David wouldn't even look at the book. He certainly wasn't interested in borrowing it. He insisted that there was no important distinction to be drawn between the religion of Islam and the ideology of Islamism. To him, the Koran was a war manual, plain and simple, and he objected when I pointed out that there was a lot about the so-called counter-jihad movement that was hurting the cause of democracy and the fight against extremism. My point was that it was one thing to reject a murderous ideology, but quite another to tell nearly two billion people that their religion was unrepentantly evil. Most Muslims around the world wanted nothing to do with the extremism of Islamist ideology. Millions of Muslims were actively involved in fighting it. They need our help, not our condemnation.

But David was having none of it. Janice didn't say a word throughout dinner. Neither did Andrew. It was worse than awkward. Andrew and

I left almost right after we'd finished eating. I knew right then my brief friendship with David was probably over. What I didn't know was that a nasty public argument was about to begin and I was about to become a pariah to the counter-jihadists.

Over the next few days, there was a flurry of emails between David and me. It started as an intellectual argument and then it turned ugly. At the same time, David was emailing our mutual friend Salim Mansur, a Muslim dissident, inclined towards classical liberalism and a University of Western Ontario political science professor, about many of the same issues that separated David's way of thinking from my own. Within a few days, David severed both of our friendships.

As I would later learn, David allowed no room for friends whose views he considered heretical, even though his own views included sympathy for the "Birther" conspiracy theory, which mainly contends that Barack Obama was born in Kenya and thus occupies the White House illegally. I was unaware of this until I came upon David in Jonathan Kay's book, *Among the Truthers*, which is about conspiracy theorists. David told Kay that "I wouldn't accept apostasy — even from a wife. I would not accept her living a lie, refusing to uncover the truth. If you can't do that, you're not my friend."

In the weeks following our dinner, a public uproar blew my disagreements with David out into the open and set me on a collision course with the counter-jihadists that also involved a great deal of grief from quite a few supporters of the Free Thinking Film Society.

The kettle was already simmering weeks before my dinner with David. I'd heard from Valerie Price, a friend in Montreal whose Act! For Canada group had occasionally hosted some of my Free Thinking Film Society guest authors at her events. Valerie told me she'd made plans to bring the British "Mosquebusters" activist Gavin Boby to Canada in February. Valerie wanted to know if I'd co-sponsor a speaking engagement for Boby in Ottawa. I was quite alarmed. I wrote to Valerie: "Could you imagine hosting someone who had an organization that was called 'synagogue busters' or 'church busters'?"

A few months before Valerie contacted me about bringing Boby to Canada, she'd attended a private "counter-jihad" mini-convention in Brussels under the banner of the International Civil Liberties Alliance. Tommy Robinson from the notorious English Defence League had attended. So had Gavin Boby, along with Ned May, an American who runs the popular anti-Islam website Gates of Vienna. Raw footage of the event had been relayed for editing and distribution to a friend of mine, the Ottawa blogger who goes by the name Vlad Tepes (our friendship would end as badly and for the same reasons as my friendship with David).

At the time, I'd warned Valerie that the EDL and Gavin "Mosquebusters" Boby were people to avoid. I clearly hadn't made much of an impression.

Boby was a British local-planning lawyer who offered free professional advice to any local council wanting help in opposing proposals for the construction of mosques. Boby pitched his services this way: "If anyone out there knows of an application for a new mosque, a cultural centre for some phoney community centre or some multi-faith inter-faith harmony institute then let me know." Boby claimed to have prevented the construction of 16 out of the 17 mosques he'd been asked to help stop. While he later disavowed his associations with the English Defence League, the EDL had "wholeheartedly" endorsed Boby's Law and Freedom Foundation and had recruited volunteers to work with him.

As for the EDL, which my former friend Vlad Tepes had devoted so much of his blog to support, I saw them as a scary bunch of racist, homophobic yobs. Vlad saw them as defending an 'English' way of life. To be fair, I understood the frustration of the people who were drawn to the EDL — successive British governments were ignoring a growing Islamist problem percolating within Britain's Muslim communities. But, it was clear to me that the EDL was repugnant and dangerous. The typical EDL protest involved rampaging through the streets, terrorizing Muslim shopkeepers and drawing hundreds of police in the effort to keep the peace. According to a BBC report, the policing of EDL marches cost more than ten million pounds from 2009 to 2013. At an EDL rally in Birmingham in July 2013, restaurants were smashed up and police were attacked with weapons. Fifty EDL members received a total of 75 years in prison.

On the phone, Valerie defended her decision to bring Boby to Canada by saying he stopped only the large mega-mosques or mosques that had ties to the Muslim Brotherhood or to Saudi Arabia. However, a quick check with Boby's website showed that he would try to stop any mosque, no matter how tiny. He'd even helped block the construction of an Ahmadiyya mosque (the liberal Ahmadiyya Muslims face vicious persecution in much of the Muslim world). Boby's bizarre legal theories include the idea that "propagating Islamic doctrine is contrary to civil and criminal law." He described his objective as "Islam going by the way of fascism and communism. It means the shrines of Islam going the way of Lenin's shrine."

Alarmed by Boby's imminent arrival in Canada, I contacted my friend Salim Mansur, the UWO professor that David Solway had disowned shortly after he'd disowned me. Salim and I co-authored an opinion piece for the *Ottawa Citizen*, titled "Mistaking Islamism for Islam." We relied heavily on Bassam Tibi's book, and stressed the point that there was a network of conservative activists in Europe and North America who were, on the surface, against Islamist extremism, but were in fact "making all Muslims and Islam their enemies."

Rather than presenting a useful ideological and intellectual challenge to Islamism, "they end up ironically supporting the Islamist view that there is no Islam other than what Islamists insist it is." By denying Muslims a role in opposing Islamism, the counter-jihad movement had "conceded the Islamist propaganda that Islamists are Islam's only legitimate representatives." We singled out Gavin Boby and his Law and Freedom Foundation, and noted that Boby had been invited to undertake a speaking tour in Canada. "We confront a hugely important struggle against Islamists. We cannot afford to get this wrong," we wrote.

The opinion piece set off a firestorm in the counter-jihad crowd.

David's partner, Janice Fiamengo, wrote to the Ottawa Citizen accusing Salim and me of being among the "privileged elite" who don't have to put up with their neighbourhoods being ruined by mosques. In the first of several denunciations he'd write in the coming days and weeks, David circulated a condemnation of Salim and me, taking us to task for our "unsubstantiated" criticisms of both Boby and the EDL. He also claimed that we'd written that "it would be ill-advised, even dangerous, for members of the public to hear Gavin Boby speak." This was obviously untrue. Toronto evangelist Mark Harding, whose polemics against Muslims had earned him a 1998 conviction under the Criminal Code's hate-crime provisions, chimed in: "Ban the Quran from Canada."

Then the Canadian Council on American-Islamic Relations (CAIR-CAN) weighed in, urging the Ottawa Public Library to rescind its permission to allow Boby to speak because it was wrong for the library to provide him with a public venue subsidized by Muslim taxpayers. Denise Fung, a producer at the CBC, asked me if I'd discuss the controversy on the local CBC morning show. She was looking for somebody to argue that the library should cancel the Boby event. But when I told her the library should let Boby's event go ahead — after all, should we just have birthday parties at the library? — Fung lost interest in putting me on the air.

Boby's talk went ahead. The Ottawa Sun quoted Boby: "When it comes to mosques, the only good thing is lots of free shoes, and they're probably not worth it." He repeated that awful joke in Montreal and Toronto, where his turnouts were also dismally small. Several Free Thinking Film Society patrons asked me why I hadn't attended Boby's Ottawa speech. Perhaps I wasn't that "free thinking" after all? I patiently answered every email, but it was obvious this wasn't going to be enough. After Boby had returned to Britain, the public arguments continued on both sides of the Canada-U.S. border and on both sides of the Atlantic. The necessary and long-overdue debate that Clifford May had wanted

Tibi's book to set off was well under way. A lot of it was nasty and mean, but this was a good thing because it brought out the worst of the "counter-jihad" movement and exposed many of the movement's leading lights as dangerously bigoted.

After he'd returned to England, Boby was helpfully explicit in his refusal to distinguish Islam from Islamism. Writing about his trip to Canada, he described himself as someone openly engaged in "anti-Islam" activism, and rejected the term Islamist out of hand as "a cowardly piece of pedantry looking for a distinction without a difference." About his talk in Toronto, he wrote: "The only thing nicer than a roomful of Islamophobes is a roomful of Zionist Islamophobes." Boby's Toronto talk had been sponsored by the Jewish Defense League. The JDL was listed as a right-wing terrorist organization by the FBI in 2001. The JDL in Canada is not, but it is just as committed to the radical ideology of Meir Kahane, whose political party in Israel, Kach and its offshoots have been banned by the Israeli government as terrorist hate groups.

In a Feb. 9, 2014, essay in the rabble-rousing American conservative webzine PJ Media, David wrote a bizarre diatribe against those of us who had come out against Boby and his ugly anti-mosque campaign. We were "affluent ideological accommodationists, socialist poobahs and progressivist conservatives dining on the calipash of slow intellection." We were in league with "political officials and administrators tainted by political correctness, media lefties, assorted members of the liberal elite, infatuated academics" and "court Jews who pride themselves on their 'social justice' credentials." Salim and I, "the emulsified tandem who published an editorial in the Ottawa Citizen," were "pseudo-intellectuals" who had mobilized "a posse of offended Muslims" against the Ottawa Public Library. Which, of course, we had not.

David also wrote another diatribe in FrontPage Magazine. He attacked Bassam Tibi by spuriously claiming that Tibi was tainted by having served as adviser to a student who'd written a thesis critical of Zionism and had gone on to turn the thesis into a book that Tibi had provided with a foreword. "It is to the detriment of their argument that

Litwin and Mansur have so naively and conveniently allowed their thinking to be shaped by this man."

A few weeks later, in May 2013, even the radical Ayaan Hirsi Ali, who was known for her acerbic excoriations of Islam as a religion, was careful to draw a distinction between Islam and Islamism in an essay published by the Wall Street Journal. Preferring the term "political Islam" to describe Islamism, Ali wrote: "What is political Islam? It is not precisely the same as the spiritual dimension of the faith. Islam is multidimensional." Political Islam derives from Islam the religion, but it "prescribes a set of specific social, economic and legal practices in a way that is very different from the more general social teachings (such as calls to practice charity or strive for justice) found in the spiritual dimension of Islam, Christianity, Judaism and other world religions."

But even this simple point was lost on a great many of the conservative activists in the counter-jihad movement. They'd never understood it. As far back as 2008, I'd noticed this in my friend the Ottawa blogger Vlad Tepes. We used to meet for coffee several times a week. Vlad always tended towards the radical, but he somehow remained a supporter of the neo-fascist British National Party (BNP) long after it was obvious what the BNP was really about. Vlad parted ways with the BNP only after I'd sent him clear proof that it was a racist organization.

It was through Vlad that I met Bjorn Larsen, who'd set up a Canadian branch of the International Free Press Society, headquartered in Denmark and founded by Lars Hedegaard. The former Marxist historian had successfully fought Denmark's hate-speech laws, and right in the middle of the uproars about Boby's visit to Canada and the opinion piece I'd co-authored with Salim Mansur in the Ottawa Citizen, Hedegaard had survived an assassination attempt at his home in Copenhagen on Feb. 5, 2013.

In October 2009, Bjorn invited several of us — at the time I was thinking of myself as part of the counter-jihad movement — to a conference on Freedom of Speech & Religion in Washington, D.C. Bjorn had hired a van and we drove down from Toronto. At first glance, the conference appeared to have some real intellectual heft. It was an International Free Press Society event co-sponsored by the Horowitz Freedom Center, and several Congressmen and Members of the European Parliament were on the agenda.

It turned out to be a gong show.

On the first day of the convention, the Texas Republican congressman Louie Gohmert started off well enough, making the case against the excesses of hate crimes legislation, but his speech degenerated into histrionics about homosexuality and pedophilia. On the second day, South Carolina Senator Jim DeMint declared it was time to "bring freedom home" and then trailed off into the ills of homosexuality and secular society. During a discussion on the limits to freedom of religion, a panelist argued the anti-evolution case for "intelligent design" and made a pitch for "social conservatism." A lot of the conference seemed scripted right out of televangelist Jerry Falwell's Moral Majority.

Bjorn didn't see anything wrong with the conference. I certainly did. When we returned to Ottawa, I wrote Bjorn a lengthy memo. I told him I wasn't interested in building some sort of coalition that only conservative Republicans would join. "Our fight is against Islamism, and we should not deviate from our target," I wrote. This wasn't supposed to be about the evils of homosexuality, socialism or public health care. It was alright to team up with American conservatives, but we should be just as open to alliances with leftists who were committed to fighting theocratic fascism and gay people who saw dangers in the accommodation of Islamic hostility to gay people. "In short, we need a lot of people on our side."

I got no response from Bjorn. I did cooperate with the International Free Press Society on bringing in Geert Wilders and Bat Ye'or to speak at events, but I didn't have much to do with Bjorn after that. But it was the Gavin Boby debacle that threw me into direct and open confrontation with the "counter-jihad" crowd.

During the uproar surrounding our Ottawa Citizen opinion piece, Salim Mansur and I decided to host events in Ottawa and Toronto devoted entirely to the subject of the distinction between Islam and Islamism. We settled on the respected conservative American author and historian Daniel Pipes, president of the Middle East Forum and publisher of the Middle East Quarterly. In Ottawa, Pipes would be joined on a panel by Salim and Brian Lee Crowley, managing director of the Macdonald-Laurier Institute. In Toronto, Pipes' co-panelists would be Salim and the National Post columnist Raymond de Souza, a Catholic priest.

Pipes was loathed by the "counter-jihad" movement and, by coincidence, immediately prior to Pipes' visit to Canada, the movement's outrageous and stridently vulgar heroine, the New York blogger-pundit Pamela Geller, was spinning at the centre of a controversy in Toronto. The Jewish Defence League was bringing in Geller to headline a public event the JDL had booked at the Chabad Flamingo Synagogue in Thornhill. This prompted the York Regional Police to warn the synagogue's rabbi that he risked losing his post as police chaplain if the event went ahead, and a huge free-speech row erupted as a result. As far as I could see, the police were acting responsibly in refusing to be associated with the JDL and Geller. Eventually, Geller's event was moved to the Toronto Zionist Centre and went off without incident, although, later on the Toronto Board of Rabbis rebuked the "radical fringe" JDL for exacerbating tensions between Muslims and Jews in Toronto.

To get an idea why the Toronto rabbis might take a dim view of Pamela Geller, a look at her obsessively anti-Islam blog, Atlas Shrugs, is sufficient. Over the years, Geller depicted Supreme Court Justice Elena Kagan in a Nazi uniform; she posted a video suggesting that Muslims are inclined to have sex with goats; a letter asserting that Malcolm X had impregnated Barack Obama's mother; and a claim that Obama had sex with a crack whore. Geller has claimed that no act of genocide occurred at Srebinica, and routinely traffics in the "birther" conspiracy theory that Obama has lied about his Hawaiian birthplace. In May 2015, Pamela Geller hosted a "Jihad Watch Muhammad Art Exhibit and Cartoon Contest" in Garland, Texas, about 20 km from Dallas; two unhinged Islamists fired at a security guard and were then shot and killed by police. Geller once again got her 15 minutes of fame, but this around, all she proved by her "free speech" event was that there was no ugly provocation that was beneath her sense of decency.

Our events with Daniel Pipes in May 2013 were well attended and Pipes' speeches were well received, despite more than a dozen "counter-jihad" activists showing up in Toronto along with a few JDL types, booing and yelling. Prior to his Ottawa speech, Pipes met privately with the Ottawa Citizen editorial board and he also wrote an opinion essay for the newspaper. His op-ed piece, titled "Islam vs. Islamism," argued that radical Islam is the problem, it's "a new variant of barbarism," and "moderate Islam is the solution." It was necessary to work with anti-Islamist Muslims "to vanquish a common scourge," Pipes wrote, "so that a modern form of Islam can emerge."

Conservative counter-jihadists were livid. Back in New York, Geller wrote: "It's hard to quantify the damage dissemblers like Pipes have done in disarming so many millions." Andrew Bostom, a professor of medicine at Brown University, a self-styled expert on Islam and a leading intellectual light of the far-right anti-Islam underworld, challenged Pipes to a debate. Pipes declined. When Pipes was back home in Philadelphia, he wrote me: "I've had lots of barrages from the left but this was a first — from the right. Unsettling it was."

A few weeks later, David Solway was back at it again. In a June 2013 essay in PJ Media, David recalled our "convivial supper," and lamented that so many people had been persuaded by Bassam Tibi's work. He wrote that I'd called Pamela Geller "a disgrace," slandered Gavin Boby as a bigot and tarred "the brave and much-defamed" Tommy Robinson of the EDL as a fascist. I'd cast suspicion on the bona fides of the controversial Dutch politician Geert Wilders and dwelled approvingly on the distinction between Islam and Islamism. "What has happened?" David asked. His former friends were falling away from the cause, "as if some sort of microbial agents has subtly infected their minds." What was under way, David complained, was a "gradual betrayal of a once-robust conservative consensus."

But if there ever was a "conservative" consensus on the subject of Islam and Islamism, it had fallen apart long before 2013.

Pamela Geller's partner-in-crime is Robert Spencer, a prolific author who bills himself as a scholar of Islam although his Master's degree in religious studies is in Catholic history. Spencer's method is to take snippets from ultraconservative Islamic texts and render them into easily understandable English. Spencer maintains that the bin Ladens of the world have got it right: their Islam is the real Islam. Just one of the most public breaks pitting counter-jihad conservatives against more thoughtful conservatives (and neoconservatives) had occurred in 2010 when such American conservative luminaries as Charles Krauthammer were roundly denouncing Dutch politician Geert Wilders as a demagogue. Spencer responded this way: "Charles Krauthammer is ignorant, naive, and wrong." Many thousands of people have read Spencer and, as a result, believe they understand Islam.

Thanks to Spencer and his fellow counter-jihadists, complex Islamic concepts like taqiya and abrogation have become standard catch phrases in conservative anti-Islam polemics around the world. Taqiya is 9th-century Shi'a practice allowing adherents to conceal their religion when under threat or compulsion. It was intended to protect minority Shi'ites in Sunni communities. Thanks to Spencer's analysis, taqiya is now routinely held up as evidence that Muslims are permitted to lie at any time in pursuit of their evil plans. The Sun Media personality Ezra Levant, in one of his defamation lawsuits, Awan v. Levant, defamed the plaintiff in the case by accusing him of taqiya in several instances.

Misinterpretations and misunderstanding like this lead us onto poisonous ground. Spreading the belief that anything a Muslim says is a lie is not just hurtful. It demolishes trust and frays the social fabric. More times than I can count, I've had people raise the "taqiya" defence against evidence of ordinary Muslims expressing peaceful, democratic views. That's what Spencer, Geller, Bostom and the rest like to do. They "dismiss the work of Muslim reformists, arguing that the only way

Muslims can bring about an enlightenment in their faith is by rejecting Islam itself," writes progressive Muslim author Tarek Fatah.

Fatah's observation is borne out by the facts. Geller: "While there are millions of moderate Muslims, there is no moderate Islam." This begs the question: What religion, then, are all those millions of moderate Muslims following? David Solway offered an answer to the puzzle in FrontPage Magazine, by explaining that these Muslims "are not really Muslims any longer, and certainly not Muslims in good standing." Rather, they are merely "nominal Muslims, dissembling members of the faith. . . engaged in a species of method acting, imagining themselves to be what they are not." That could have been Osama bin Laden talking.

With pronouncements like those, David Solway, Bostom, Spencer, Geller and the rest were mimicking Islamism. I'd been noticing this in the "counter-jihad" for quite some time. They were agreeing with the bin Ladens of the world that their version of Islam was correct. They were agreeing with theocratic fascists like the Egyptian Islamist scholar Yousuf al-Qaradawi, the godfather of the Muslim Brotherhood. They were saying that al-Qaradawi's understanding of Islam was better than anybody else's, and that Islamist theologians were the only credible spokesmen for Islam. They aren't.

There is much to be said for observations writers and critics like Bruce Bawer and Ayaan Hirsi Ali make about the troubling nature of central aspects of the Muslim faith itself. There is also no doubt that there is much to be concerned about in the growth of enclave communities of Muslim immigrants in Europe, originating in Bangladesh, Pakistan and North Africa. Many of these communities have been incubating some of the worst excesses of "Islamic" practices and backward cultural values that pose grave challenges to liberal democracies. It is also true that Islamism derives from Islam, but these two things are not the same.

The contemporary ideology of Islamism emerged from the wreckage of the Ottoman Empire and the Islamic Caliphate at the end of the First World War. Islam descended into the depths of a crisis of confidence that had been afflicting Muslim societies for at least a century.

Out of the Ottoman ashes, the Muslim Brotherhood was born in 1928, and the Brotherhood would go on to incorporate into its ideology the philosophy of Sayed Qutb, who is arguably the father of contemporary Islamism. Qutb, who was hanged in Egypt in 1966 for his part in a plot to assassinate Egyptian president Gamel Abdul Nasser, but not before he'd written a 30-volume series, In the Shade of the Qur'an, which built the foundations for Islamism as an ideology and jihad as a religious duty.

Paul Berman's *Terror and Liberalism* provides an important analysis of Qutb's works, and Berman's later book, *Flight of the Intellectuals*, focuses on the inability of western intellectuals to properly understand the phenomenon of Islamism, particularly its apocalyptic aspects, its anti-Semitism and its seductive totalitarianism. Far from being merely a religion, Islamism is an ideology that anticipates a "vanguard of true Muslims" making a clean sweep of the Muslim religion. That vanguard is called upon to "turn against the false Muslims and 'hypocrites' and do as Muhammad had done, which was to found a new state, based on the Koran," Burman writes. "And from there, the vanguard was going to resurrect the caliphate and take Islam to all the world, just as Muhammad had done."

This will require "a total dictatorship" of theocrats, in the same league as "the other grand totalitarian revolutionary projects of the 20th century," like Nazism and Communism. To Qutb, "Crusaders" and Zionism posed mortal threats to Islam. Followers of the "false Islam" that most Muslims practiced would have to be brought under the strict rule of sharia, the law of the Koran, in order to restore the lost caliphate. Religious campaigns against the kuffars (disbelievers) are obligatory, all lands formerly under Muslim rule must be recaptured, any peace treaty with outside enemies must be broken, and Muslims who defy the new order should be considered apostates and put to death.

The virulent anti-Semitism that usually goes hand in hand with Islamist ideology was largely imported into the Arab world from Christian Europe. The historian Bernard Lewis in *The Jews of Islam* wrote, "In Islamic society hostility to the Jew is non-theological." But

Islamism's seething hatred of Jews, according to Robert Wistrich, author of *Anti-Semitism: The Longest Hatred*, derives partly from Ottoman-era blood libel myths, partly from 19th century Christian influences in the Arab world, and most significantly, from the success of Nazi propaganda during the 20th century. The Nazi-allied Grand Mufti of Jerusalem, Hajj Amin al-Husayni, was a key trafficker in Nazi-propagated myths about Jews.

In his book, *Nazi Propaganda for the Arab World*, historian Jeffrey Herf details how a continual stream of anti-Semitic Nazi propaganda into Arab countries beginning in 1939 combined selective readings of the Koran with Nazi denunciations of western imperialism and Soviet Communism. The combination of genocidal anti-Semitism with the anti-Judaic verses of the Koran made for a poisonous toxin. Mix all that with Islamist exhortations to jihad and you have a recipe for disaster.

That's what Islamism is. It is not Islam the religion and it is not the faith of nearly two billion Muslims, no matter how hard the conservative counter-jihad movement tried to make it out to be. Neither is it a "legitimate" or "understandable" reaction to the NATO intervention in Afghanistan, to the U.S. invasion and occupation of Iraq or to the "western imperialism" that the "anti-war" movement said it was — the lies that had disgusted me about the "left" all those years ago.

This is how the counter-jihadist conservatives were so very much like the so-called "liberals" that emerged as the loudest voices in the months and years following 9/11. The Pamela Gellers and the Robert Spencers were just as willing as the Noam Chomskys and the Michael Moores to conflate Islam with Islamism, to conflate ordinary and devout Afghans with the Taliban, and to conflate the totalitarian, niqab-enforcing Wahhabi culture of Saudi Arabia with the religious customs of the overwhelming majority of the world's innumerable Muslim faith communities.

Just one instructive example of this conflation was on display in the responses of both Opposition leaders in Ottawa to an almost casual remark by Prime Minister Stephen Harper in March 2015. Harper had used the term "anti-woman" to describe those cultures that require women to wear the full-body, face-covering shroud of the niqab. Liberal leader Justin Trudeau responded by saying Harper needed to explain to Canada's half-million Muslim women "why he said their chosen faith is anti-women" when Harper had said nothing about the faith traditions of the majority of Canada's Muslims. NDP leader Thomas Mulcair said Harper was referring to "a culture of 1.8 billion human beings as being anti-woman," when Harper was talking about nothing of the kind.

This is what the "counter jihad" conservatives share with what I ended up calling the "postmodern left." The counter-jihad conflation of Islamism and Islam would want "the west" in constant war with nearly a fifth of humanity, or would otherwise surrender the world's Muslims to the mercies of the totalitarian Islamists — the Taliban, Boko Haram, Hamas, Hezbollah, the Khomeinists, Al-Qaida, the Islamic State, and on and on. The "postmodern left" would also abandon the world's democratic, liberal and reformist or otherwise moderate Muslim majority by its pursuit of peace, co-existence or outright capitulation to the Islamist totalitarians.

That's a lot of collateral damage to tolerate in the western world's encounter with Islam, and if the counter-jihadists had their way, the fallout wouldn't be suffered only by Muslims.

In Europe, one of the counter-jihadists' anti-Muslim tactics is to ban or limit access to halal foods. But if you limit or stop the production of halal food, notably beef products, then you also stop or limit the availability of kosher food to Jews. Geert Wilders' PVV Party in the Netherlands has considered a ban on ritual slaughter as well as a ban on the import of kosher meat from abroad. Understandably, this has prompted a protest from the Netherlands' chief rabbi. Right-wing parties in Germany have also proposed a ban on the Muslim (and Jewish) custom of circumcision. A leading counter-jihad website, Gates of Vienna, editorialized in August 2012 that "if Jews cannot in good conscience abide by the law of the land, then yes, they may want to move to Israel — and thank God they have that choice!" The editorial concluded: "To turn on Geert Wilders over this issue, after all his years of supporting the Jews and Israel, shows a distressing lack of perspective."

In November 2013, the internet was rife with rumours that the government of Angola had banned Islam. Geller approved, writing that it was "self-preservation on a continent where countries are getting swallowed whole by jihadists enforcing the sharia. It's a defensive move." Spencer, who loves his own freedom of speech, wrote on his blog that Angola's move was "clearly" just a national security issue and "there is no way in Angola any more than there is anywhere else to distinguish jihadis in Angola from the peaceful Muslims among whom they move, organize and recruit, and clearly this measure is designed to stop that activity." Only after the story was exposed as a hoax did Spencer decide that an Angolan ban on the Muslim faith would be contrary to "freedom of conscience."

The counter-jihad crowd also always asks, just where are all the moderate Muslims? As if there weren't any. In fact, they're everywhere.

In Canada, there are about 60 different ethno-cultural Muslim groups — proof of the immense diversity of the Muslim community. There are Iranian-Canadians actively opposed to the thuggish regime of Islamist clerics in Tehran. In 2013, thanks to their efforts, the Canadian Parliament unanimously passed a resolution to commemorate the 25th anniversary of the slaughter of thousands of political prisoners by the Khomeinist regime. Similarly, Afghan-Canadians were overwhelmingly supportive of Canada's involvement throughout the years of the NATO mission in Afghanistan. Pakistani Canadians have been very active in their opposition to the brutality of Islamist groups in Pakistan, and have also protested the Pakistani government's ruthless oppression of the Baloch minority. Bangladeshi-Canadians constantly raise funds to support activists in Bangladesh who are engaged in confrontations with Islamists back in the old country.

During the Parliamentary debates on the fight against ISIS, Defence Minister Jason Kenney pointed out in a speech to the House of Commons: "In the last two days we have been visited in Ottawa by leaders of the Canadian Iraqi, Syrian, Chaldean, Yazidi, Kurdish, Shia, secular Sunni, Arab communities, all of whom have enthusiastically endorsed the motion before the House on the extension and expansion of the Canadian military operation against this genocidal terrorist organization. I emphasize the word genocidal."

The Arab Spring, denigrated by many of the conservative counter-jihad crowd as proof of the immutability of Islam, was in reality proof of the opposite. Much of the hopes of the Arab Spring have been crushed by Islamist and police-state repression, but it hasn't all been negative. After their revolution, Tunisians freely voted in a non-Islamist government. Before their abandonment by the NATO countries took its toll, Libyans confirmed a progressive constitution and elected liberals and anti-Islamists to its provisional government. Hundreds of thousands of Egyptians took to the streets to show that they were not content to be ruled by the Muslim Brotherhood. They overthrew the regime of Mohamed Morsi. In Syria, the mass uprising that was later engulfed in Baathist and Islamist mass murder was a pro-democracy movement.

When French troops helped liberate Mali from the grips of an Al-Qaida offshoot, who can forget the celebrations of the Malian people? They were delirious with joy and their first thought was to bring out the beer. Or how about the trials in Bangladesh of the Islamists who murdered thousands of people? Nine leaders of Jamaat-e-Islami, the largest Islamist party in Bangladesh, were put on trial, convicted and sentenced. What about the tens of thousands of Iranians who took to the streets in 2009, protesting the votes stolen by Mahmoud Ahmadinejad that year? And who will ever forget the courageous Kurdish fighters who have bravely fought ISIS?

The anti-Islamist right conveniently overlooks the majority of Muslims who live outside of the Middle East, too. Hundreds of millions of Muslims in the Indian subcontinent, in Indonesia and Malaysia practice forms of Islam far different than the Wahhabism of Saudi Arabia that oppresses so many people throughout the Arab world. In 2007, Maulana Jamil Ilyasi, president of the All India Organisation of Imams and Mosques, led a delegation on a visit to Israel. His group represents about 500,000 imams and nearly 200 million Indian Muslims, just fewer than 15 per cent of the global Muslim population. "The time for violence has come to an end, and the era of peace and dialogue between Muslims and Jews has begun," Ilyasi said, adding that Pakistan should establish diplomatic relations with Israel.

In 2007, Abdurrahman Wahid, the former president of Indonesia and the spiritual leader of Nahdlatul Ulama, an Islamic organization with roughly 40 million members, told Bret Stephens of the Wall Street Journal that the "only solution" to Islamism in Indonesia was "more democracy." Wahid said his mission was to "discredit Islamism's ideology of hatred." When Wahid died in September 2009, flags were at half-mast in Indonesia for seven days.

Wahid wrote the foreword to Paul Marshall and Nina Shea's book, *Silence: How Apostasy & Blasphemy Codes Are Silencing Freedom Worldwide*, which would be published two years after Wahid died. He wrote: "Rather than legally stifle criticism and debate — which will only encourage Muslim fundamentalists in their efforts to impose a spiritually void, harsh, and monolithic understanding of Islam upon all the world — Western authorities should instead firmly defend freedom of expression, not only in their own nations, but also globally, as enshrined in Article 19 of the Universal Declaration of Human Rights."

It's not that hard to find liberal voices even in the harsher societies of the Arab world. Nasser Weddady and Sohrab Ahmari profiled several anti-Islamist dissidents in their 2012 book, *Arab Spring Dreams*. Dalia Ziada, a 24-year-old Egyptian woman who started the annual Cairo Human Rights Film Festival, was developing civil rights programs in Egypt. There was Tarek Shahin, a 23-year-old Egyptian cartoonist who pokes fun at politics in Egypt; Farea al-Muslimi, an 18-year-old Lebanese student fighting for press freedom; S. Murshid, a young girl in Syria who worked with the Committee for Defending Freedom and Human Rights; and B. al-Mutair, a 25-year-old Kuwaiti, an activist for democracy in her country.

In Malmo, Sweden, the young Muslim Siavosh Derakhti set up the group "Young People Against anti-Semitism and Xenophobia." The Egyptian writer and playwright Ali Salem says Israel is a friend to Egypt and that the real enemy is Hamas. The Egyptian blogger Maikel Nabil Sanad delivered a speech at Hebrew University in Jerusalem: "First of all I came to say a peace-seeking community exists in Egypt, even as the media is trying to make it look like there isn't. We oppose war and are pro-peace with all countries including Israel." The Syrian rebel leader Muhammad Badie personally thanked Israeli Prime Minister Benjamin Netanyahu for setting up a field hospital for Syrians wounded in the civil war. Several Syrian rebel leaders sent congratulatory notes to Netanyahu when he won re-election in March 2015.

In Canada, anti-Islamist Muslims Raheel Raza and Salim Mansur founded the Muslims Facing Tomorrow group to oppose "extremism, fanaticism and violence in the name of religion" and to "advance among Muslims the principle of individual rights and freedoms." Other Canadian groups are Tahir Gora's Muslim Committee Against Antisemitism in Toronto, Tarek Fatah's Muslim Canadian Congress and Salma Siddiqui's umbrella group, the Coalition of Progressive Canadian Muslim Organizations.

"If Islam is to truly thrive, it will only do so when more and more anti-Islamist Muslims confront and extinguish radical Islamist ideologues," the British Muslim Qanta Ahmed, daughter of Pakistani immigrants, wrote in the Times of Israel in January 2013. "Otherwise, we stand to lose both Israel and Islam in one fell swoop of the Islamist axe. Whether rescuing Palestinians and Israelis captive to the whim of Hamas, or rescuing Islam from Islamist Hamas, this is truly our jihad and no one else's, which is why Israel's jihad is also mine."

You'll never hear about these voices from the anti-Islam right and its counter-jihad propagandists. They'll never let on about the width and depth of resistance to Islamism amongst Muslims. You'd never know about the work of anti-Islamist Muslims helping police forces thwart the many terrorist attacks attempted by Islamists in North America. You'd never hear a thing about the overwhelming majority of Afghan Muslims who bravely resisted the Taliban and supported the NATO intervention.

You'd never know any of these things from listening to the "anti-war" movement, either. To the counter-jihad "right," it was always simple: Blame Islam. To the anti-war "left," it was just as simple: Blame America.

By 2014, I'd made up my mind. A pox on both their houses.

Postscript

I was always the skeptical one. At Passover Seder, when the door was opened to welcome the angel Elijah, I wanted to know if he really drank some wine from the cup left on the table for him. One year — I must have been eight or nine — I decided to put some tape on his glass and see if the wine went down after the door was opened to welcome him. Everybody at the table seemed somewhat alarmed, and there were attempts to divert my attention while someone moved the tape. I thought it was a good scientific experiment. I was puzzled that no one else at the table shared my enthusiasm.

Being Montrealers, Passover was a time when our Jewish religion clashed a bit with our Montreal Canadiens religion. The Stanley Cup final would often coincide with Passover so there was no way we could watch the game. The compromise was to keep the TV on in my grandparents' den, run in every now and then and whisper the latest score around the table while my grandfather conducted the service.

As I look back at where I've been and where I am now, what I find striking is that I really haven't changed all that much. My socialism, back in the 1980s, made me passionate about the need to topple dictators and to liberate people around the world. I'm no longer a socialist. I've done well for myself as a capitalist. But I still strongly believe that freedom, liberty and democracy are universal values that all people will ultimately want.

I never would have dreamed that one day I'd end up joining a conservative political party, but when I look back, maybe I'd become accustomed to contradictions just by growing up Jewish in Montreal in the 1960s. At the time, the public schools were still divided into the

Protestant and Catholic systems. The Jews went to Protestant schools. Until I was in Grade Seven, the half-hour Bible study (always the New Testament) was replaced by a "civics" class. We started our day with "O Canada" and "God Save the Queen." Then we said the "Lord's Prayer." Sometimes we recited the 23rd Psalm: "The Lord is my shepherd, I shall not want. . ." Every day we sang two hymns from the Protestant hymn book.

If you can picture me as a 10-year-old singing Onward Christian Soldiers, then maybe it will be easier to picture me in the 1980s as a Bay Street investment analyst by day and an organizer for the movement against Canada's involvement in the U.S. cruise missile program by night. That might help explain, too, why it was possible for me to join the Conservative Party. I became a conservative without abandoning the Jewish and progressive values I grew up with — the importance of alleviating poverty, caring for people and fighting for equality and against discrimination. And I made many good friends in the Conservative Party. I worked for some mighty fine candidates. Unfortunately, by the time I sat down to write this book, the Conservative Party had come to feel like an ideological strait-jacket. The Conservative Party had become more concerned with the Conservative Party than with ordinary people. I'll probably let my party membership lapse.

To be fair, the Harper Conservatives proved to be fairly competent, and they did several important things: tax-free savings accounts; ultimately balancing the budget after the deficits from the 2009 recession; reforming immigration and refugee policy; a cold shoulder to oil company takeovers by Chinese state-owned enterprises; and the signing of several free-trade agreements.

But there are a host of problems that need government attention, and the Conservatives ended up seeming mostly absent.

Take the issue of the CBC. While the Conservatives have cut the budget of the CBC by about 10 per cent, they have refused to set any strategic direction for the state-owned broadcaster. Some of my conservative friends have strenuously argued that the CBC should be privatized, but that's not my view. I believe that the CBC should operate like PBS in the United States, and be supported mostly by its viewers and listeners. But the whole debate is entirely academic since the Conservatives won't take any bold steps to change the CBC. They'll just let it list with the wind.

You'd think the Conservatives really cared about the military, but that just wasn't true. While NATO has set a goal of two per cent of GDP for defence spending, Canada was down to less than one per cent during the Conservatives' final years. According to historian Jack Granatstein, that's the lowest since the 1930s. Australia was spending $30 billion per year on defence compared to our $20 billion. And military procurement was in huge trouble — the F-35 purchase was completely mishandled and we have not yet started to build the ships we need — the new icebreaker will only enter service in 2022. More than $10 billion was returned to the treasury because it couldn't be spent.

Other files just languish. Even files that are "conservative" in nature are ignored. You'd think the Conservatives would get rid of supply management, but it was a Liberal, Martha Hall Findlay, who actually made the first serious proposals for change. And there were many other issues they ignored: They wouldn't simplify our taxes and eliminate corporate welfare. They wouldn't fix the broken family law system and end blatant discrimination against fathers. They seemed unable to sign any new treaties with aboriginal people, or make any headway on the deeply dysfunctional aboriginal affairs file. They let the Senate dangle and the House of Commons sink further into irrelevance. Private experimentation in health care was out. They couldn't care less about the shape of Canada's capital city. Equalization couldn't even be mentioned. Bilingualism was off-limits, along with any discussion of moving back towards the merit principle in hiring.

The Harper Conservatives were actually quite timid. One might even say arrogantly timid.

Internationally, they'd become very vocal about supporting Israel and Ukraine, and they'd denounce Putin any day of the week, but in the end they know they don't have to do much. It's nice to see the Harper government send 200 troops to help train Ukrainian forces, but surely we can do better than that. Even our contribution to the coalition against ISIS was somewhat tepid, with six CF-18s, one tanker, one surveillance plane and 69 Special Forces Troops. Tiny New Zealand has sent 143 Special Forces troops and the Netherlands and Belgium sent six F-16s each.

Harper's Canada spoke loudly and carried a twig.

We could be very thankful that our Conservatives are very different from the American conservatives, though.

I attended the February 2015 Conservative Political Action Conference (CPAC) in Washington, D.C. What a mess.

The three-day event featured speeches from all the major Republican presidential candidates, breakout sessions on a variety of topics, a trade show of conservative NGOs and a number of private parties and dinners. Among the potential Republican candidates were Ben Carson, Governor Chris Christie, Senator Ted Cruz, Governor Scott Walker, Governor Bobby Jindal, Senator Marco Rubio, Governor Rick Perry, Carly Fiorina, Donald Trump, Governor Jeb Bush, and Senator Rand Paul. There were also fringe, off-the-wall conservatives like Governor Sarah Palin, UK Independence Party leader Nigel Farage, and television's Duck Dynasty patriarch, Phil Robertson.

Each of the prospective presidential candidates said much the same thing. It was like ordering from a menu at an old Chinese restaurant, with a few twists: Take everything in Column A (I support traditional marriage, I am pro-life, I love guns), choose three from Column B (America is the freest/greatest country on earth, God is still blessing America, only in America can an immigrant be successful, I love the constitution and will defend the balance of powers, I believe in American exceptionalism, America's best days are in front of us, we need new ideas), and Column C (I oppose legalization of marijuana, I support Israel, ISIS must be destroyed, We must tighten the border, Repeal Obamacare, I will balance the budget, I will strengthen the military, time to cut taxes, I will fix the education system), and choose one from Column D (Abolish the IRS, stop EPA regulations, defund Planned Parenthood, establish term limits, and reform entitlements).

It was all platitudes with very little detail on anything. And there was a major contradiction between belief in American exceptionalism and the stated goal of defeating ISIS. Bret Stephens, the Wall Street Journal foreign affairs columnist, notes in his book, *America in Retreat: The New Isolationism and the Coming Global Disorder*: "Exceptionalism is a call for introspection, not action; for apartness, not engagement: it offers at least as strong a case for isolationism as it does for internationalism or interventionism."

And while I was appreciative of the support for Israel, I heard very little on how ISIS would be defeated exactly, or how they would stand up to Vladimir Putin, or how they would stop the mullahs of Iran. Wisconsin's Scott Walker told delegates he had the stuff to beat ISIS because he had taken on the unions. With everybody talking about cutting taxes and cutting programs to balance the budget, it was difficult to understand how the military could be rebuilt or how the United States could play a bigger role in the world.

Of course, the isolationist Rand Paul was somewhat different. He preached "Ron Paul light" libertarianism combined with Chomskyite isolationism, but underlying all his talk of freedom was just plain nuttiness. He once tweeted about an article on Alex Jones' loony conspiracy website Infowars about the National Weather Service allegedly stockpiling 46,000 hollow-point bullets (the bullets were in fact for a separate bureaucracy's fisheries enforcement officers). Paul once blasted the Senate Foreign Relations Committee for voting to arm elements of the Syrian opposition saying "you will be funding, today, the allies of Al-Qaida," which was another lie. He'd also suggested a link between vaccines and a variety of mental disorders. In 2009, he called mandatory vaccines a step towards "martial law," and he was caught in a February 2012 video claiming that the United States was partially to blame for causing World War II by provoking Japan.

Donald Trump told delegates that when it came to border security, he was the man because no one could build a wall like him. Duck Dynasty's Phil Robertson claimed that 110 million Americans were sick with sexually transmitted diseases: "I don't want you, America, to get sick. I don't want you to become ill. I don't want you to come down with a debilitating disease. I don't want you to die early." Fortunately, Sarah Palin gave a heavily scripted speech about veterans and her teleprompter held.

Whether it was John Boehner or Mitch McConnell or Michelle Bachmann, all the leading Republicans gave me the creeps.

I could understand the anger that drew people to the so-called Tea Party — after all, Obama had racked up almost eight trillion dollars in debt and right after the financial crisis, he spent $800 billion on a variety of partisan projects that combined a huge amount of pork. The Tea Party wanted America to turn inward, to radically remake the United States into a patchwork of small-minded states with little national purpose. The libertarian right would like the United States to not only drastically cut the military but to continue the retreat begun under Barack Obama.

And Republicans continued to embarrass themselves when they talked about homosexuality. In May 2014, Representative Charles Van Zandt of Florida said that the Common Core (a set of Federal educational standards) would "attract every one of your children to become as homosexual as they possibly can." In June 2014, Texan Republicans voted to support "reparative therapy" for gay people. In March 2015, Ben Carson told CNN that homosexuality was a choice because of the behavior of prisoners. Fortunately for the Republicans, the U.S. Supreme Court ruling legalizing same-sex marriage takes the issue off the table for the 2016 election. Even so, candidates like Ted Cruz and Scott Walker have proposed a variety of constitutional amendments to turn back the ruling, which led conservative columnist George Will to write that "Sixteen months before the election, some candidates are becoming too unhinged to be plausible as conservative presidents."

But, how about the Canadian left?

In spite of all the years that have passed since September 2001, the NDP's base was still weighed down by an outmoded, anti-colonialist, "anti-imperialist" view of the world, which was all on display at the August 2014 People's Social Forum in Ottawa. The event was sponsored by most of Canada's major public sector unions — CUPW, CUPE and PSAC — as well as well as the Ontario Federation of Labour, the Canadian Labour Congress, Confédération des Syndicats Nationaux (CSN), Centrale des Syndicats du Québec (CSQ) and some private sector unions, like Unifor, Canada's largest private sector union, the United Steelworkers, and others. Rabble.ca was also a sponsor of the event. Participating organizations included the Council of Canadians, Independent Jewish Voices, Idle No More Quebec, No One is Illegal Toronto, Ontario Coalition Against Poverty, Alternatives, Canadian Dimension, and the Coalition against Israeli Apartheid.

The four-day event featured more than 500 seminars, a Unity March and Rally, a film festival, several concerts, a children's festival, 19 movement assemblies, six caucuses (people of colour, original peoples, etc.), a healing space, kiosks, vendors, an alternative media centre, an indigenous friendship centre, a people of colour welcoming space, a pow wow to kick off everything and a convergence assembly to end the Forum. More than 3,000 people attended. The 100-page program noted that participants were "dedicated to sharing an oppression-free space" and were expected to conform with certain guidelines: "When witnessing or experiencing racism, sexism, etc., interrupt the behavior and address it on the spot," "Keep space open for anti-oppression discussions; try focusing on one form of oppression at a time — sexism, racism, classism, etc.," "Be conscious of how your language many perpetuate oppression," "promote anti-oppression in everything you do, in and outside of activist space," "Avoid generalized feelings, thoughts, behaviors, etc. to a whole group."

Among the seminars: Strategies for lesbian workers in the face of heteronormativity in the workplace; Veganism in the Occupied Territories: anti colonialism and animal liberation; Using Hip Hop to deconstruct Justice Issues; Marx was right!; Theatrical ritual and collective identity: the fantasy of community; Caucus for people with experience selling or trading sex; How to get climate change warning labels on gas pump nozzles in your community; Fear of a Black Planet: Anti-Black Racism & Misogynoir in our Movements; Anarchy 101; Building the anti-imperialist peace movement; Combating Rape Culture on Canadian Campuses; Sacred Water Circle – Leading with prayer walking together for solutions and action; Five decades of the Cuban Revolution; Combining gender and anti-racist educations to better address misogyny, effeminophobia, homophobia & racism.

A star speaker at the event was Naomi Klein. The forum newsletter, Gaggle, noted: "Journalist Firzoe Manji challenged Klein on her use of the phrase 'extraction industries' and instead asked her to consider fossil fuel development in terms of 'amputation.'" Other speakers included Malalai Joya, Linda McQuaig, Maude Barlow, Judy Rebick, Brigette Depape, Sid Ryan, Ariel Troster, and Yves Engler.

Several seminars on Israel and Palestine were predictably hostile to the Jewish state. The convergence Assembly on Palestine and the Palestinian people, organized by a variety of boycott, divestment and sanctions advocacy groups, turned into a competition to see who could add the most militant text to the final declaration. The Assembly called for the boycott, divestment and sanctions against Israel and an end to the occupation of the West Bank, the Golan Heights, East Jerusalem and Gaza. It also demanded the right of return of all Palestinian refugees to their homes in Israel (which would mean the end of a Jewish state). The so-called "right to resist by whatever means they [the Palestinians] choose," a not-so-veiled attempt to support indiscriminate violence like Hamas missiles, passed as well. There was not one word friendly to the Jewish people or to Jewish Israelis.

I attended several seminars.

The seminar on Ecofeminist struggles for a post fossil-fuel, democratic society took the cake. It was conducted by Terisa Turner, a former sociology and anthropology professor at the University of

Guelph. She wanted a world that had turned back to animal-driven carts. She claimed that Chevron left Nigeria after women put on a "Show Your Vagina" demonstration. I asked her if this strategy could defeat Boko Haram and she said it was complicated: The Muslims have been pushed into a small area where they have no books or schools and so they have no choice but to join Boko Haram, which in any event is financed by the CIA, as was the Taliban.

There might very well have been some important ideas at the Peoples' Social Forum but everything was couched in postmodernist jargon and identity politics. After the event was over, Rabble published an article by Steffanie Pinch, their "activist toolkit" coordinator, with the headline "Calling out whiteness at the Peoples' Social Forum." Pinch complained about the Forum's "overwhelming whiteness." The article prompted a response from the Forum organizers, complaining about the article: "All four main coordinators were People of Colour or Indigenous; further, nearly half of steering committee members were PoC or Indigenous." The coordinators explained: "If white people truly want to deconstruct the white hegemony that benefits them and harms PoC and Indigenous communities, then the question must be asked: why do we consistently fail to build long-lasting relationships? The fact remains that many silenced and oppressed people — PoC, Indigenous, Queer, differently abled etc. — choose not to engage in events because we are tired of constantly having to defend ourselves and justify our experiences."

As for the main currents of Canadian politics, back in 2011 the columnist Andrew Coyne had written an opinion piece in Maclean's Magazine calling for a new federal political party, and his arguments had resonated deeply with me. "By now it will have occurred to many people that there is something deeply sick about our national politics. . . Politics in this country — federal politics, at least — is in a kind of death spiral, whose terminus is not dictatorship but irrelevance. It exudes a sense of anomie, a corrosive cynicism that is not just indifferent to principle but hostile to it."

To Coyne, the "two big gaps" were "political decency" and "political seriousness." Coyne was right on the money. The platforms of our political parties are not worthy of a great democracy, and Parliament was a "pantomime" where very little was getting debated.

When I was a delegate at the 2008 Conservative policy convention in Winnipeg, a motion came to the floor to allow the provinces to experiment with private health care. Stephen Fletcher, who had been the Parliamentary Secretary to the Minister of Health, went to the microphone and delivered a strong plea to defeat the motion — not because it was a bad idea, and not because the provinces should not have the right to experiment. It was because if it passed, the Conservatives would be perceived as hostile to national health care, and that would be unacceptable. Fletcher handily won the day. Style won and substance lost.

The odds of any new political party along the lines Coyne raised seem very, very slim. The federal Liberals could have reinvented themselves after the 2011 election. They could have outflanked the Conservatives on the "right" on certain issues and outflanked the NDP on the "left" on other issues. They could have decided to tackle issues no other party would touch. Instead, they elected Justin Trudeau, a pretty boy with a famous name whose main work experience prior to being elected to Parliament was a part-time drama teacher at an expensive private school.

If a new party was to emerge, there are quite a few things I'd want it to tackle. A return to the merit principle in hiring. Work with the provinces to try and recover universities from their post-modern morass. Fix our broken family law system to end arbitrary discrimination against fathers. Implement a guaranteed annual income program to help the poorest of Canadians get a step up. Simplify and flatten the tax system. End corporate welfare. Create a new pension system so that everybody can retire in dignity. Reform the civil service so that people aren't sick and depressed and actually look forward to work. Refocus the CBC so that it serves all Canadians. Allow the provinces to experiment with private health care. Implement a national dental care program. Enable aboriginal independence. Empower the committee system in Parliament. Revisit the federal Status of Women mandate to ensure that men's issues finally get some attention.

But mostly, Canadians should be allowed to thoroughly re-evaluate their country's place in the world. There's a huge international void waiting to be filled.

We'd need to begin by letting go of the idea of Canada as a nation of "peacekeepers" and "honest brokers." When I was growing up, we were proud of our place in the world. We were the inventors of peacekeeping and Canada could always be counted upon to take a leading role in UN missions. But our physical role in peacekeeping missions has been on the decline since 1995, when the Liberals were in power (Canada still makes significant funding contributions to UN peacekeeping).

In 1990, Canada had about 1,000 peacekeeping troops in place, and it had declined to 130 in 2006 and 34 in 2014. We now rank 65th in the world in peacekeeping. That era is now over, and we are no longer required to supply the UN with blue-helmeted peacekeepers. There is now a greater need for troops and personnel ready to fight for peace and against the forces of fascism, to train police and military forces, and to forge the way for humanitarian aid in disaster and war zones around the world. We were never "honest brokers," anyway, if that term means "neutral" or "uninvolved." Yes, Lester B. Pearson won a Nobel Peace Prize in 1957 for his work in the Suez crisis, but we still took a clear side in that conflict, as we did throughout the Cold War.

The United States, under Barack Obama, has been in full retreat from the world. It doesn't look like any Republican successor would behave very differently. Countries like France may be called on to step up to the plate. The French led the successful effort to depose Libyan dictator Gaddafi in 2011, and the French defeated Al-Qaida forces in Mali in 2013. As Conrad Black put it in his 2014 book, *Rise to Greatness: The History of Canada from the Vikings to the Present*, Canada is not going to be able to replace the United States in the world — "no country could do that" — but there is an opportunity and a duty for Canada "to fill some of the space that has been vacated."

Canada is in a fairly good position to pick up some of the slack America's retreat has created. Our finances are in good shape. We aren't burdened by the sclerotic lethargy of most western European countries. We also have credibility that few can match, largely because we have no overseas colonial baggage and no history of unjust wars. And despite what the NDP sometimes says, the world thinks well of Canada.

The Harper Conservatives once sensed that Canada could play a bigger role in promoting democracy. Their 2008 platform stated that they would "make the promotion of Canada's democratic values on the world stage a major focus of our foreign policy." The Conservatives pledged to establish "a new, non-partisan democracy promotion agency that will help emerging democracies build democratic institutions and support peaceful democratic change in repressive countries."

That never happened.

In 2011, the Liberal Party promised: "We will establish a Canada Democracy Agency, with capacity to broker, coordinate and support deployments of Canadian governance expertise, from both within federal agencies, and beyond — including other governments, retired professionals, the private sector and NGOs."

And why on earth shouldn't Canada lead big time on this issue? How about also pushing for a Council of Democracies — an organization that could have far more relevance, far more clout and far more gravitas than the ridiculous, dictator-driven United Nations?

Canada could lead on democracy and freedom around the globe. We could be the ones to champion dissidents around the world and to help oppressed minorities everywhere in their fight for freedom. As dictators fall, and they inevitably do fall, Canada could be the first in to help build fledgling democracies.

It wouldn't be easy. We'd have to stare down China and promote Taiwan, actively support the Iranian opposition, organize international coalitions, tell the Saudi royal family to keep its brand of Wahhabism to itself, and occasionally we'd have to remind the Americans about their own commitment to human rights.

Want the CBC to do something useful for a change? How about CBC Farsi to unite Iranians around the world? Sure beats *Little Mosque on the Prairie*, no?

Further, the government must offer more opportunities for Canadians to match significant international initiatives. In 1979, the government introduced a matching program for the acceptance of Vietnamese boat people into Canada, and more than 60,000 Vietnamese refugees were allowed into the country, far more than originally planned. Matching programs are routinely used for relief projects but their use can be extended to educational, social and other uses, too. We also need to get more Canadian schools and communities involved.

Alaina Podmorow is a Canadian hero. She started raising money for teachers in Afghanistan when she was nine years old. As of 2015, her charity, Little Women for Little Women in Afghanistan, had raised more than half a million dollars. Twelve-year-old Craig Kielburger, from Thornhill, Ontario, started an NGO, "Free The Children," to work against child labour. Think of what could have been done if every grade school in Canada had been paired with a grade school in Afghanistan. When kids get involved, creativity flourishes and the emotional involvement is at a very deep level. Cities and towns can also be twinned to help our foreign policy goals. Civic engagement easily trumps the bureaucrats sitting in Ottawa.

Changing the national narrative to one based on freedom and democracy will also bring together leaders and activists from a broad cross section of Canadian minority communities. Their concerns, interests and experiences — in short, their solidarity — in ongoing struggles against totalitarian, authoritarian and anti-democratic regimes and forces in their homelands, could enrich our foreign policy. Relearning the importance of solidarity not only helps with Canadian cohesion, but can help fight apathy, ameliorate the isolation that new Canadians often experience, and provide ways for far-flung diaspora communities to learn from one another, to share experiences and ideas, and build alliances and partnerships in peace, order and good government, and the global cause of democracy, equal rights and the rule of law.

When it comes to winning the Olympic Gold Medal in hockey, there's nothing this country won't do. When Canada excelled at the 2010 Vancouver Olympics, we all took pride that we were the first host nation to lead in Gold Medals since Norway in 1952 — our 14 Golds set a new record. But we were all a bit sheepish about our "Own the Podium" slogan. It was a bit brash for us. Many in the international community were also taken aback — was Canada going too far for Olympic success? Wasn't this completely out of character?

It's time for us to be brash. And if we are going to brash about something, then why not for freedom and democracy?

Acknowledgements

Andrew Yip has stayed by my side throughout twists and turns and the ups and downs of my journey. He was always there to help at Free Thinking Film events and he always helped with a smile. Thank you, my dear partner.

I want to thank Terry Glavin for his tremendous help in editing and shaping this book; few people in Canada know this material better than Terry. Tamara Fulmes and Roy Eappen have been my partners in crime at the Free Thinking Film Society and I thank them for their wisdom and advice. Jamie Ellerton came up with the idea for the Fabulous Blue Tent, and both Roy and I were delighted to work with him. Thanks, Jamie, for the spirit and drive that actually moved gay rights forward more than most people in the gay intelligentsia.

Other people to thank include Barbara Kay for always being supportive; Mark Collins who teaches me something every time we meet; Shelley Crowley for always making me laugh (or cry); Peggy Berkowitz for advising me to travel back in 1983 when I was somewhat adrift; Salim Mansur for teaching me more about humanity and compassion than I ever thought possible; my sister Sandra Levy and my brother-in-law Ron Levy for opening their house and hearts to Andrew and me; all of the Yips (Rick, Jennie, Karen and Jill) who have warmly welcomed me into the family; Harry Weldon for teaching me the value of civic engagement; Paul Reddick, who is Canada's poet-laureate of the blues; Michael Sona for his courage and integrity; Daniel Richardsen for his inspiration; and many others who have inspired me along the way — Keith Fountain; Bruce Bawer; Don Cummer; Brian Lee Crowley, Joseph Ben-Ami, Lynne Ben-Ami, Gerry Toomey; Ricky Stevens; Delroy

Dyer; Danno Saunt; Georganne Burke; Zeek Gross; Richard Marceau; Scott Simon; Raheel Raza; Anthony Fulmes; Charles Swindle, John Acton, David Kilgour, Watermelon Slim, JW-Jones, Tom Lacey, Lionel Phang, Sjarif Ismail, Salma Siddiqui, Anna-lee Chiprout, Brent Beatty, Jeffrey Asher, Barry Godin, Judd Silverman, Michael Mostyn, Jeremy Swanson, Marjorie Hansen, Shameer Ramji, Damian Konstantinakos, Emyrs Graef, Leesha Cunningham, Pu Chen, Richard Wong, Peter Cho-Wing, Nicolas Fleet, Charles Kaine, Ron Radosh, Michael J. Totten, Paul Michaels, Bob Plamondon, and Daniel Wiener & Tingwen Wang.

Any error or mistake is mine and mine alone.

Notes and Sources

I really want to thank the Canadian Gay and Lesbian Archives, located in Toronto, for their help in providing copies of Capital Xtra from 2001 to 2008. I know of no place in Ottawa that has a complete set of Capital Xtra newspapers.

Many of the speakers who have appeared at Free Thinking Film Society events are online at YouTube.

All of my Access to Information (ATIP) requests can be found online at the websites of the various departments involved. If you want to receive any of these documents, you can repeat the same ATIP request for just $5.

For updates, review and pictures about this book, please visit conservativeconfidential.com

Introduction

The RCMP and the identification of homosexuals: Daniel J. Robinson and David Kimmel, "The Queer Career of Homosexual Security Vetting in Cold War Canada, Canadian Historical Review, March 1994.

The Fruit Machine: Artifact number 19990189-001, Canadian Museum of History.

Treatment for homosexuality in Alberta: "Alberta doctors continue to bill province for treating homosexuality as a mental disorder akin to pedophilia," National Post, February 24, 2012.

Chapter 1: The World Turned Upside Down

Police and firefighters: Christie Blatchford, "This triumph of the spirit belongs to men," National Post, September 22, 2001.

David Horowitz, *The Politics of Bad Faith: The Radical Assault on*

America's Future (Simon & Schuster, 1998).

AIDs cases in Canada: Public Health Agency of Canada, HIV and AIDs in Canada, Annual Surveillance Report.

Anti-Zionist campaigns of the Soviet Union: Robert Wistrich, A Lethal Obsession: Anti-Semitism from Antiquity to the Global Jihad (Random House, 2010). See Chapter Three: The Soviet War Against Zion.

The Oslo Peace Process: Dennis Ross, *The Missing Peace: The Inside Story of the Fight for Middle East Peace* (Farrar, Straus and Giroux, 2004).

Durban NGO Forum Declaration: See Article 426, http://www.i-p-o. org/racism-ngo-decl.htm.

"Indifferent to the suffering": Haroon Siddiqui, "Dear Neighbours," Toronto Star, September 13, 2001.

"American complicity": Haroon Siddiqui, "Tough Balancing Act for Bush," Toronto Star, September 19, 2001.

"This is not the war of democracy": Robert Fisk, "The wickedness and awesome cruelty of a crushed and humiliated people," The Independent, September 12, 2001.

"in the course of which it worked with, armed and trained – Osama bin Laden": Rick Salutin, "One Way to Beat the Bombers," Globe and Mail, September 14, 2001.

"had anything to do with the recent UN conference": Susan Riley, "At times like this, we thank God that we're Canadians," Ottawa Citizen, September 12, 2001.

"the conditions in which such twisted logic": Naomi Klein, "Game Over: The End of Video Game Wars," Globe and Mail, September 14, 2001.

Complete text of Sunera Thobani's Speech: "The Speech That Shook The Country," Sunera Thobani, http://www.herizons.ca/node/131.

Michel Chossudovsky, "Osamagate," Globalresearch.ca, October 9,

2001.

Noam Chomsky, *9-11* (Seven Stories Press, 2001).

Chapter 2: Into The Wilderness

Netanyahu at Concordia: Sara Ahronheim, "Eyewitness to Hatred: Concordia University, Montreal," http://www.israelnationalnews.com/Articles/Article.aspx/1356#.VVtTTEb4JB8, September 13, 2002.

Israel Apartheid Week started in Toronto: Avi Weinryb, "The University of Toronto – The Institution where Israel Apartheid week was Born," Jerusalem Center for Public Affairs, December 24, 2008.

Chomsky visit to Toronto 2002: Alice Klein, "Bless His Soul," NOW Magazine, November 14, 2002.

Jean Chretien CBC interview: "PM links attack to 'arrogant' West," National Post, September 12, 2002.

Carolyn Parrish on the "influence of the Jewish lobby": Al-Ahram Weekly Online, 29 August – 4 Sept. 2002, http://weekly.ahram.org.eg/2002/601/re6.htm.

Heather Mallick quote on Carolyn Parrish: Heather Mallick, "There are Americans I love. Really," Globe and Mail, November 22, 2004.

David Collinette quote: "PM links attack to 'arrogant' West," National Post, September 12, 2002.

CBC debate on the use of the word terrorism: Norman Spector, "Dear Peter Mansbridge: When will CBC finally use the 'T' word?" Ottawa Citizen, December 21, 2002. Reply by Tony Burman, Ottawa Citizen, January 2, 2003.

Saeb Erekat on 500 Palestinians killed in Jenin: Jonathan Steele, "The Tragedy of Jenin," The Guardian, August 2, 2002.

Concordia University Students Union's 'Uprising' Magazine: 2001 Audit of Antisemitic Incidents, League for Human Rights of B'nai Brith Canada.

The Makuya: Also called Makuya of Christ, is a Christian movement that began in 1948. Their students reside at the Heftziba Kibbutz, where I stayed for about three months in 1984.

Saddam Hussein payments to suicide bombers: Chris McGreal, "Saddam Funds fail to buy Gaza hearts," The Guardian, March 13, 2003.

Tommy Franks on being told by King Abdullah that Saddam Hussein had WMD: "Retired Gen. Tommy Franks Says U.S. Should Put Iraq on 5-Year Plan," PR Newswire, July 30, 2003.

Tommy Franks on being told by Mubarak that Saddam Hussein had WMD: Carl Limbacher, "Gen. Franks: Iraq had WMDs in 2003," Newsmax.com August 4, 2004.

Bill Clinton on unaccounted "biological and chemical" material left in Iraq: Bill Clinton on CNN on July 22, 2003, as quoted in the Congressional Record, V. 149, PT. 14, July 17, 2003-July 23, 2003.

Anti-war rally in Victoria, B.C. in 2003: Audit of Antisemitic Incidents 2003, League for Human Rights of B'nai Brith Canada.

Anti-poverty rally in Toronto in 2003: Audit of Antisemitic Incidents 2003, League for Human Rights of B'nai Brith Canada.

The Hidden Tyranny on Indymedia: http://portland.indymedia.org/en/2002/05/11568.shtml

Cairo Declaration 2002 and signatories: http://pubs.socialistreviewindex.org.uk/isj98/rees.htm

Cairo Conference 2003: http://www.mdsweb.jp/international/cairo_sec/cairo2_dec.html

Ramsay Clark and Ma'moun El-Hodeibi of the Muslim Brotherhood at Cairo Conference: "American Anti-War Movement Leaders Meet with radical anti-Zionists in Cairo," Anti-Defamation League, December 29, 2003.

Protests to adding PFLP to Canada's terror list: "Open Letter to

Solicitor General of Canada Re: Banning of Palestinian Groups," website of the Canada Palestine Association, November 21, 2003, http://www. cpavancouver.org/index.php/2003/11/21/open-letter-to-solicitor-general-of-canada-re-banning/.

"Challenging Canada's Role in Empire" Conference: The complete conference agenda is at this web site, http://www.nowar-paix.ca/cpa/cpaprogram.pdf

Adbusters: Ron Csillag, "Jewish 'neocons' tilt U.S. policy toward Israel, says magazine," Canadian Jewish News, April 8, 2004.

Bush visit to Canada: Thomas Walkom, "Should Canada Indict Bush?" Toronto Star, November 16, 2004.

Elizabeth May on George Bush: http://www.vivelecanada.ca/article/11212998-black-ribbons-for-bush-protest.

George Bush hostage to "hawks": Haroon Siddiqui, "Is U.S. really serious about ending carnage in Mideast?" Toronto Star, April 14, 2002.

Osama bin Laden trained by CIA: Haroon Siddiqui, "Learning large lesson of the war on terrorism," Toronto Star, December 23, 2001.

Civil liberties of American Muslims suspended: Haroon Siddiqui, "Imperial U.S. war machine is on the move," Toronto Star, September 29, 2002.

Bush on a holy mission: Haroon Siddiqui, "Bush's credibility on line," Toronto Star, June 5, 2003.

Syria is accused: Haroon Siddiqui, "Two years after 9/11 attacks, a report card," Toronto Star, September 7, 2003.

Gore backed by Jewish-American voters: Haroon Siddiqui, "In 'new' Middle East, Saddam isn't the enemy," Toronto Star, February 18, 2001.

Khomeinist Iran electing moderates: Haroon Siddiqui, "Learning large lessons of the war on terrorism," Toronto Star, December 23, 2001.

Claims about Khomeinists interfering in Afghanistan: Haroon Siddiqui,

"Bellicose Bush pushing his luck with coalition," Toronto Star, February 10, 2002.

"Unapologetic support for those resisting Israeli occupation": Ibid.

Linda McQuaig 150 columns for the Toronto Star: These are available using its archives.

"Linda McQuaig says moving closer to US promotes war," April 24, 2005.

"Linda McQuaig says today's charade is simply about Iraq's oil," January 30, 2005.

"Bush sells sizzle in war on terror," April 4, 2004.

"Pliable Bush puppets of hawks," March 16, 2003.

"Rebuffed President recklessly saddles up for war," March 9, 2003.

"The thing is, it is about oil," February 16, 2003.

"U.S. wants to liberate our energy," April 20, 2003.

"Africa suffers, West chants mantra of trade, not aid.," June 30, 2002.

Statistics on Rabble, ZMag and The Nation websites: Catherine Porter, "Tell me more – Hungering for more information since Sept. 11, people are turning to alternative media for other views on the news," Toronto Star, November 20, 2001.

The enslavement of the Iraqi people by Texans: Heather Mallick, "I liked it so much I bought the country," Globe and Mail, September 27, 2003.

The Bush cult: Heather Mallick, "How to greet the guy next door," Rabble.ca, November 29, 2004.

Chapter 3. A New Home

Andrea Dworkin: She died on April 9, 2005. My lunch with Peggy was six days later.

Fahrenheit 9/11 is "convincingly argued": Geoff Pevere, "9/11 film places real issues in spotlight," Toronto Star, June 25, 2004.

"Secure and Protect" the Bush family interests: Ibid.

"a major political rethink": Haroon Siddiqui, "Long arm of the law nabs Bush," Toronto Star, July 8, 2004.

"I hope this doesn't happen": Peter Howell, "Thorough Bushwhacking," Toronto Star, June 19, 2004.

"Get ready to send your kids": Ibid.

Fahrenheit 9/11 claims: David T. Hardy & Jason Clarke, *Michael Moore is a Big Fat Stupid White Man*, (Reganbooks, 2004).

Florida election: Dennis Cauchon, "Newspapers' recount shows Bush prevailed," USA Today, May 15, 2001; Ford Fessenden & John M. Broder, "Study of Disputed Florida Ballot Finds Justices Did Not Cast the Deciding Vote," New York Times, November 12, 2001.

Unocal: Christopher Hitchens, "Why Bush Conspiracy Theories Don't Add Up," Daily Mirror, June 30, 2004.

"while rich, private interests benefit": Linda McQuaig, "Moore Misery for the U.S.," Toronto Star, July 11, 2004.

Bush speech at Alfred E. Smith Memorial Foundation Dinner: "A Pause for Humor" PBS New Hour website, Transcript - http://www.pbs.org/newshour/bb/politics-july-dec00-alsmith_10-20/

Manufacturing Dissent: Debbie Melnyk, "On the Moore Watch," Sunday Telegraph, April 18, 2007.

Unlocked doors in Sarnia: Tony Allen-Mills, "Tables turned on Fahrenheit 9/11's maker," Times Online, March 4, 2007.

State Farm Insurance Survey: Joyce Walder, "The No Lock People," New York Times, January 13, 2010.

"If Michael Moore had his way…": Christopher Hitchens, "Unfairenheit 9/11: The Lies of Michael Moore," Slate, June 21, 2001.

Fahrenheit 9/11 ticket sales: Edward Jay Epstein, "Paranoia for Fun and Profit: How Disney and Michael Moore cleaned up on Fahrenheit

9/11," Slate, May3, 2005; http://www.slate.com/articles/arts/the_hollywood_economist/2005/05/paranoia_for_fun_and_profit.html.

Anthony Chernushenko letters: You can find his letters on the internet. For example, he wrote this: It appears at this stage to be very unlikely that President Bush will be able to escape the smothering embrace of the US Christian Right and the pro-Israel lobby. Nor is it at all likely that he will want to do so. He would be left out in the cold. -- Anthony Chernushenko, Ottawa, Canada on the German website DW-World in reply to the article, "What can the world expect from Bush II?"

The problem with the Conservatives: http://gayandright.blogspot.ca/2005/12/problem-with-conservatives.html

Seven Issues the Conservatives won't touch: http://gayandright.blogspot.ca/2005_12_01_archive.html

Michael Moore on the Canadian Election: http://mcadams.posc.mu.edu/blog/Moore_Canada2.htm

Chapter 4. Iranium

Obsession the movie: http://www.obsessionthemovie.com/

"An Obsession with protests": Denis Armstrong, "An Obsession with protests," Ottawa Sun, January 25, 2007.

Mine your own Business: http://www.mineyourownbusiness.org/

Indoctrinate-U: http://en.wikiquote.org/wiki/Indoctrinate_U

Cinema Politica: http://www.cinemapolitica.org/ottawa

Ottawa Xpress Review of Che film: http://ottawaxpress.ca/2008/07/10/free-thinking-film-society-deconstructing-che/

Ottawa Xpress Review of The Case for Israel: http://ottawaxpress.ca/2009/04/09/free-thinking-film-society-a-fine-imbalance/

Ottawa Xpress Review of Media Malpractice: http://ottawaxpress.ca/2009/06/11/free-thinking-films-media-malpractice-twisting-the-lens/

Mark Leiren-Young's interview of Michael Moore: http://ottawaxpress. ca/2009/10/01/michael-moores-capitalism-a-love-story-moore-from-michael/

Ezra Levant – Elizabeth May debate: https://www.youtube.com/ watch?v=hwnCobh4roA

Iranium: http://www.iraniumthemovie.com/

Source for the timeline of events at the Library & Archives Canada: In 2012, I submitted two Access to Information requests to the Library and Archives Canada (A2011-00576, Cancellation of the event "A Window to the Sun's Land"; and A2011-00523, Cancellation of the film *Iranium*). I also submitted one Access to Information request to Heritage Canada (A2011-00253, Cancellation of the film *Iranium*). I received a total of 985 pages between the three requests, and I used these documents to recreate a timeline of events within the Library & Archives Canada.

Number of blog posts about Iranium: Email message from the *Iranium* producers dated January 24, 2011.

Ottawa Citizen report on the Iranian Embassy request to cancel Iranium and the denial from the Library & Archives Canada: Robert Sibley, Kristy Nease and Sneh Duggal, "Film cancelled after Iranian request," Ottawa Citizen, January 19, 2011.

CBC report in which the Library & Archives deny cancelling Iranium twice: http://www.cbc.ca/canada/ottawa/story/2011/01/19/ottawa-iranium-cancellation.html

A Window to the Sun's Land: Lee Berthiaume, "Iranian event at Library and Archives also cancelled," Embassy Magazine, February 16, 2011.

"already-sour" relations between Canada and Iran: Ian Macleod, "Documentary spat worsens Canada-Iran relations," Ottawa Citizen, January 20, 2011.

Ottawa Citizen opinion essay: John Mundy, "The issues behind the controversy," Ottawa Citizen, February 5, 2011.

Worry that Heritage had violated arms-length relationship: Jamie Portman, "Moore was wrong to force Iranium showing," Ottawa Citizen, January 25, 2011.

"false flag" operation: http://yayacanada.blogspot.com/2011/01/false-flag-at-national-archives.html

"BigCityLib": http://bigcitylib.blogspot.ca/2011/01/on-cancelling-iraniums.html

"Fred Litwin is happy as a pig in the proverbial cesspool": http://drdawgsblawg.ca/2011/02/inanium.shtml

$15,000 security costs: This was a figure provided to me by one of the top security officials at the Library and Archives Canada.

Quote from Iran's External Affairs ministry: Shar Bani, "Iran regime's warning about the Iran-phobia movement in Canada," Voice of America, February 11, 2011; http://www.voanews.com/persian/news/Iranium_Mehmanparast-2011-10-02-115731154.html.

Iranium at York University: Sarah Boesveld, "Protests at York University's Iranium Screening," National Post, February 11, 2011.

Booking of Library & Archives auditorium: From an ATIP request previously cited.

$1,920 fee for the use of the archives: Email from the Library & Archives Canada to the Free Thinking Film Society.

Chapter 5. Stephen Harper's Holy War on Homos

Manhattan Declaration: You can see the full text of the Manhattan Declaration at its website, www.manhattandeclaration.org

Joseph Farrah: "WND Drops Ann Coulter from Miami Event Over Homoconflict," WND website, August 17, 2010; http://www.wnd.com/2010/08/192405/#LClEDcWek1sCRvXr.99.

Coulter response: "Brian Montopoli, "Ann Coulter Dropped from Conservative Conference over Participation in Gay Republican Event 'Homocon,'" CBS News, August 18, 2010.

Log Cabin Republicans History: www.logcabin.org

Elsie Wayne: "Elsie Wayne speaks up on gay marriage," CBC News, January 3, 2006.

James Murphy letter: Capital Xtra, May 22, 2003.

Andrew Sullivan, *Virtually Normal: An Argument about Homosexuality* (Alfred A Knopf, 1995).

First issue of The Body Politic: Nov/Dec 1971.

Gerald Hannon, "Of Men and Little Boys," The Body Politic, Issue 5, August 1972.

Gerald Hannon, "Men loving boys loving men," The Body Politic, Issue 39, December 1977/January 1978.

The Body Politic closes in 1986: "Body Politic to cease publication," Toronto Star, December 23, 1986.

First issue of Capital Xtra: Brandon Matheson, "Blazing a new trail," Capital Xtra, September 24, 1993.

Rex Wockner history of Pink Triangle Press: Rex Wockner, "Never sucking up," Capital Xtra, December 7, 2001.

Xtra West and court challenges: Eleanor Brown, "The arrogance of Egale," Capital Xtra, September 14, 2001.

Anger about gay community embrace of marriage: M. Anne Vespry, "Is that all there is?" Capital Xtra, July 14, 2005.

Conspiracy theory: M. Anne Vespry, "Road Tripping with Zero," Capital Xtra, November 3, 2005.

"lamented the victories on the same-sex marriage front": Pat Croteau, "What about respecting polyamorous gays?" Capital Xtra, July 14, 2005.

"Marx and Engels were decidedly gloomy": Maryusa Boclurkiew,

"Privatizing Our Sex Lives: Same-sex marriage is just not enough, thank you," Capital Xtra, September 28, 2006.

PTP founder Charles Dobie: Fred Kuhr, "The $200 that started it all," Capital Xtra, December 21, 2006.

Ariel Troster objecting to anti-homophobia advertising campaign: Ariel Troster, "Don't pity me," Capital Xtra, April 5, 2007.

Gareth Kirkby opposition to same-sex marriage: Gareth Kirkby: "Marriage fight a waste," Capital Xtra, October 18, 2007.

The case of Dale Eric Beckham: "Web luring case raises age-of-consent issue," CBC News, March 8, 2005.

Vic Toews' long time fantasy: Paul Gallant, "A jackboot for Vic Toews," Capital Xtra, February 27, 2006.

"teen sex rights": "Age of consent by country," Capital Xtra, March 15, 2006.

Fred Litwin letter to the editor: "Age of Consent Series Offends," Capital Xtra, April 13, 2006.

Other letter writer: Paul Larocque, "Appalling Letters," Capital Xtra, April 13, 2006.

"police the decisions of queer youth": Andrew Brett, "Hands out of my pants," Capital Xtra, August 17, 2006.

NDP 2006 convention: Andrew Brett, "How the NDP screwed their own queer youth," Capital Xtra, September 21, 2006.

Gareth Kirkby on the NDP: Gareth Kirkby, "NDP & Liberal cowards," Capital Xtra, February 28, 2008.

"the Conservatives are a scary bunch": Gareth Kirkby, "Remember this image," Capital Xtra, June 23, 2004.

Right before the 2004 election: Julia Garro, "'Unnatural' progress," Capital Xtra, June 23, 2004.

In May, PTP publisher David Walberg: David Walberg, "Wipe that smirk," Capital Xtra, May 26, 2004.

After Harper lost to Liberal Paul Martin: Blaine Marchand, "Better to face the devil you know," Capital Xtra, August 12, 2004.

March 2005 Conservative policy convention in Montreal: Gareth Kirkby, "Right vs Wrong," Capital Xtra, April 7, 2005.

"Monsignor Harper": Gareth Kirkby, "Monsignor Harper's biblical oratory," Capital Xtra, May 19, 2005.

"the article set a new standard for shrillness": David Walberg, "Harper's Holy War," Capital Xtra, January 26, 2006.

For more on the supposed threat of the Christian right in Canada: Marci McDonald, "The Armageddon Factor," The Rise of Christian Nationalism in Canada (Random House Canada, 2010).

"When a chorus of boos went up": Ariel Troster, "Putting up a fight," Capital Xtra, April 17, 2006.

"the spectre of Harper using his power of judicial appointments": Brenda Crossman, "Judges with Bibles," Capital Xtra, September 21, 2006.

"Harper conning his own constituency": Jared Mitchell, "Harper's motion made him no friends," Capital Xtra, October 21, 2006.

Several months after the gay marriage debate: Marcus McCann, "60 Reasons to dump Harper," Capital Xtra, May 29, 2007.

Canadian troops should be brought home: Gareth Kirkby, "Bring our troops home," Capital Xtra, April 23, 2008.

During the Persian Gulf War in 1991: Compiled by Paul Gallant, "Pink moments," Capital Xtra, September 11, 2003.

First Capital Xtra column after 9/11: Blaine Marchand, "Unpredictable Acts of Violence," Capital Xtra, October 12, 2001.

Anti-terrorism legislation "should have us all concerned": Brenda Crossman, "Perhaps you're a terrorist," Capital Xtra, November 14, 2001.

"modern day fight against terror where it's hard to separate the good

guys from the bad guys": Ariel Troster, "James Loney sets an example," Capital Xtra, April 13, 2006.

Two months later, Troster was at it again: Ariel Troster, "Does injustice make you feel safe?" Capital Xtra, June 8, 2006.

Double page spread in November 2006: Krishna Rau, "Welcome to THE SECURITY STATE," Capital Xtra, November 30, 2006.

Final issue of Capital Xtra: Feb 12 – March 11, 2015.

The holy war could just be around the corner: Mathew Hays, "How Xtra magazine came to the end of the rainbow," Globe and Mail, February 20, 2015.

Chapter 6. The Fabulous Blue Tent

Dr. Dawg's blog: http://drdawgsblawg.blogspot.ca/2008/11/sore-thumb-chronicles-blue-fog-journey.html

Jaime Watt denounced: Krishna Rau, "Gay leaders denounce Egale award to Jaime Watt," Capital Xtra, June 4, 2009.

Bruce Bawer, *Surrender: Appeasing Islam, Sacrificing Freedom* (Doubleday, 2009).

Bruce Bawer, *A Place at the Table: The Gay Individual in American Society* (Simon & Schuster, 1993).

Bat Ye'or, Eurabia: *The Euro-Arab Axis* (Farleigh Dickinson University Press, 2005).

Private Sponsorship of Refugees (PSR) Program: Details on the meeting in Vancouver came from an Access to Information Request (A2013-10166) to Citizenship and Immigration Canada.

Birth of QuAIA: http://queersagainstapartheid.org/who/

Jeremy Dias writing on Israel Apartheid: see Montreal Kiosk, "Controversy over the term "Israeli Apartheid" plagues Toronto Pride," http://www.montrealkiosk.com/magazine-r-g.php. The same article was in the Montreal gay guide, 2B Magazine.

Article on the Ottawa Police Gay Liaison Committee: Noreen Fagan, "Police in Hot Water Again," Capital Xtra, November 11, 2010.

"kick off a Pride Toronto-calibre meltdown in Ottawa": Marcus McCann, "On policing, gays forge ahead," Capital Xtra, November 11, 2010.

Fabulous Blue Tent: http://fabulousbluetent.ca

It Gets Better Video: https://youtu.be/ZV1i8LWb9hY

Open letter to Stephen Harper: Rob Salerno, "Open Letter to Stephen Harper," (Capital Xtra, October 21, 2011).

Dewar on John Baird: Lee-Anne Goodman, "Will the Real John Baird Stand Up Now?" Huffington Post, February 3, 2015.

Stephen Harper at Commonwealth meeting in Trinidad: Tristin Hopper, "Warrior for gay rights: The Conservatives have become unlikely LGBT supporters," National Post, September 22, 2012.

Baird speech to Royal Commonwealth Society: Jeff Davis, "John Baird points finger at gay rights abuses in African, Caribbean countries," National Post, January 23, 2012.

Jason Kenney's email: "Jason Kenney's mass email to gay and lesbian Canadians," CBC News, September 25, 2012.

Troster complains email is homonationalism: Glen McGregor, "Jason Kenney's office mined web petition to target message to gay Canadians," National Post, September 24, 2012.

Charge of Pinkwashing: Glen McGregor, "Kenney's emails targeting gay community raises privacy concerns," Ottawa Citizen, September 25, 2012.

Refugees accepted into Canada on the basis of sexual orientation: Access to Information Request (A2014-03941) to the Immigration and Refugee Board of Canada.

Capital Xtra was similarly apoplectic: Justin Ling, "Jason Kenney's gay email," Capital Xtra, September 24, 2012.

Response from Kenney: Ibid.

Capital Xtra complaining about John Baird's criticism of Putin: Andrea Houston, "Come out of the closet if you want to help Russian gays, activists tell John Baird," Capital Xtra, August 8, 2013.

Kathy Shaidle: Her blog, five feet of fury, contains a steady stream of anti-gay invective. She often writes of the so-called Gay Agenda (get five gays together and we couldn't even agree on lunch), and seems to think it is impossible for gay people to have long-lasting loving relationships. Here is the link to her posting on "we want butt sex": http://www.fivefeetoffury. com/2010/01/09/6581/#BHpE6krk8tOejB9G.99.

Matthew Hays, "Is Canada run by a gay mafia," Vice.com, July 5, 2013.

Michael Coren, "I was wrong," Toronto Sun, June 28, 2014.

Survey of evangelicals on same-sex marriage: Elizabeth Dias, "How Evangelical are changing their minds on gay marriage," Time Magazine, January 15, 2015.

Mormons and anti-discrimination laws against LGBT: Maria La Ganga, "An embrace that swayed the Mormon Church on gay rights," Los Angeles Times, January 31, 2015.

Laura Payton, "'Fabulous blue tent' showcases gay Conservatives' power", CBC News, December 30, 2013).

"emergence of the neoliberal queer": Jonathan Valelly, "An altered activism," DailyXtra, January 30, 2013.

Gary Kinsman website: www.radicalnoise.ca

Ariel Troster, "Sex work. Our struggle," Capital Xtra, February 20, 2008.

Marcus McCann, "The Unfinished Project of gay activism: 25 battles still being fought," Capital Xtra, July 7, 2011.

Andrea Houston, "WorldPride organizers concerned about 'pinkwashing,'" Capital Xtra, June 27, 2013.

Vancouver Queer Film Festival: Lauren Kramer, "Film fest accused of 'pinkwashing,'" The Canadian Jewish News, September 4, 2014.

Susan G. Cole, "WANTED: A queer leader who knows community and can build bridges," Xtra, January 29, 2011.

Storm into straight bars: Ariel Troster, "Plant the flat," Capital Xtra, August 16, 2007.

Deep Lez: Ariel Troster, "Pitching my tent on inclusive ground," Capital Xtra, March 15, 2007.

"the right kind of porn": Julia Gonsalves, "Finding the right kind of porn," Capital Xtra, December 21, 2006.

"hypothetical lesbian household": Julia Garro, "The freedom to conform is not freedom at all," Xtra, November 23, 2006.

"something abnormal about their pussies?": Julia Gonsalves, "Is your pussy pretty enough?" Capital Xtra, September 21, 2006.

"taught spectators to expect it": John Sinopoli, "Back in the Buff," Capital Xtra, June 11, 2003.

"acknowledge cisgender privilege": Ariel Troster, "What I learned on summer vacation," Capital Xtra, September 6, 2007.

Fred Litwin appearance on "The Agenda": http://theagenda.tvo.org/episode/206640/living-out-there

QuAIA disbanding: Sue-Ann Levy, "No surprise QuAIA disbanding," Toronto Sun, February 27, 2015.

Ali Abunimah quote: Ali Abunimah, "Toronto queer group that won right to say 'Israeli apartheid' wraps up," The Electronic Intifada, February 27, 2015.

Chapter 7. You Need a Documentary for that?

Canadian Institute for Jewish Research Conference in 2011: http://www.isranet.org/cijrs-international-conference-combatting-delegitimation-israel

IPSOS/Reid Poll from 2010: In 2012, I filed seven Access to Information requests to the CBC and I received more than 3,000 pages of documents.

O'Leary's comment on Chris Hedges: Cassandra Szklarski, "O'Leary's 'nutbar' remark breach of policy, CBC ombudsman says," Globe and Mail, October 14, 2011.

"sweeping survey": "New-look CBC aims for the hip," Toronto Star, January 6, 2006.

Jennifer McGuire quote: Bruce DeMara, "CBC courting younger ears with changes," Toronto Star, March 19, 2007.

"Unlike some other CBC hipsters": Vinay Menon, "Media seek youth market: Strombo is the real deal," Toronto Star, February 15, 2005.

Guests on Strombo's show: I received a 40+ page document from the CBC with a full list of his guests through an Access to Information request.

George Galloway on The Hour: You can see his first appearance on the show at this link: https://youtu.be/uzg2Fpm0QlU

George Galloway's speech in Gaza: https://youtu.be/IYFGIbaabTU

George Galloway's subsequent appearance on George Stroumboulopoulos Tonight: https://youtu.be/67cvp_8UG34

Ayaan Hirsi Ali appearance on On The Map: https://youtu.be/08EYqwyns-k

Alastair Crooke: For more information on Crooke's Conflict Forum see Michael Weiss and Hussein Ibish, "The ex-spy who stepped into the cold," The Daily Star, July 29, 2011.

Crooke appearance on On The Map: https://youtu.be/oDvGaEeefBU

Ann Jones appearance on On The Map: https://youtu.be/4iihtd8TDjo

Ayaan Hirsi Ali appearance on Q: https://youtu.be/4jisYWdj_HU

Michael Moore appearance on Q: http://www.cbc.ca/news/arts/q-interview-michael-moore-1.995705

Michael Scheuer: The CBC provided me a list of all appearances by Michael Scheuer on CBC public affairs shows through an Access to Information request filed in 2014 (A2013-0012).

Eric Margolis on the CBC: You can see the results of a complaint about Eric Margolis in the CBC Ombudsman's review for 2012. http://www.ombudsman.cbc.radio-canada.ca/en/complaint-reviews/2012/identification-of-guest-commentator/

Michael Scheuer testifying before Congress: https://youtu.be/XHl1JnQoIWQ

Assassination of Obama and Cameron: You can read Scheuer's essay at his website. http://non-intervention.com/1146/the-desperate-u-s-uk-relationship-barack-obama-david-cameron-and-the-nsagchq-issue/

Scheuer on bin Laden and his foreign policy alternatives: David Frum, "Michael Scheuer's Meltdown," The Daily Beast, January 3, 2014.

"criticizing Israel in the United States is like a martyrdom operation": http://www.memritv.org/clip/en/867.htm

Michael Scheuer, *Marching Towards Hell* (Free Press, 2008), pp. xiv

Esther Enkin on Eric Margolis: This is from an Access to Information request to the CBC.

Sale of Jamieson Pharmaceuticals: Ellen van Wageningen, "U.S. firm buys Jamieson for $300M," The Windsor Star, January 27, 2014.

Margolis on no evidence linking bin Laden to 9/11: "9/11. The Mother of all Coincidences," (Taken from Margolis' website: http://ericmargolis.com/2010/09/911-the-mother-of-all-coincidences/.

Margolis on Israel assassinating Yasser Arafat: "Yasser Arafat," November 15, 2004, http://www.bigeye.com/fc111504.htm.

Margolis and the American Conservative magazine: Margolis wrote the cover story, "The March to Folly" about Iraq for the first issue of the magazine in October 2002.

Tony Burman columns for the Toronto Star:

"Charlie Hebdo: the case for not reprinting," January 17, 2015.

"Iran Steps UP, leaving Canada, Israel alone," June 21, 2014.

"Time for Canada, Israel to stop living in a fantasy world," January 18, 2014.

"Iran's critics, full of sound and fury," November 16, 2013.

"America ripe for a new revolution," October 19, 2013.

"Peace in Syria requires Iran, not bombing," September 7, 2013.

"Canadian extremism – we're wrong on Iran," June 22, 2013.

"Invading Iran: why resistance is now crucial," November 12, 2011.

"Ottawa unwise to echo Netanyahu," September 7, 2012.

Burman prediction on war in the middle east: Tony Burman, "Why there will be a war in the Middle East this year," Toronto Star, January 21, 2012.

Burman on Netanyahu as Canada's "new foreign minister": Tony Burman, "What has prompted Canada's move against Iran?" Toronto Star, September 7, 2012.

HonestReporting Canada 1,000 complaints to the CBC: Testimony of Mike Fegelman, Executive Director of HonestReporting Canada to the Standing Senate Committee for Transport and Communications, October 28, 2014.

Sun News on Mulroney opera: Brian Lilley, "CBC flushed Mulroney cash away," Toronto Sun, April 18, 2011.

Sun News on Hubert Lacroix expenses: Brian Lilley, "CBC Stars in own expense drama," Ottawa Sun, February 20, 2014.

This Hour Could Have 10,000 Minutes: Details for ordering the documentary are at this website. http://gayandright.blogspot.ca/2012/01/

this-hour-could-have-10000-minutes.html

Canada and the Lobby, Radio-Canada documentary: http://ici. radio-canada.ca/emissions/une_heure_sur_terre/2010-2011/exclusif. asp?idDoc=158443

As It Happens broadcast in 2009 on Israeli war crimes: Vince Carlin, Review from the Office of the Ombudsman, "Alleged war crimes during Gaza Incursion," March 20, 2010.

January 27, 2011 Power & Politics: Letter from Esther Enkin, CBC News Executive Editor, released under an Access to Information Request to the CBC (A2011-00179).

Ahmadinejad threatening to wipe Israel off the map: Ibid. See also the Review from the Office of the Ombudsman, "'Wipe Israel off the map' translation controversy," October 30, 2009.

The New Great Game: http://www.cbc.ca/player/News/TV+Shows/ The+National/ID/2291441893/

John Baird on Power & Politics regarding Vivian Bercovici: The CBC Ombudsman, Esther Enkin, said in her review that her religious affiliation was "acceptable to raise in the context of the interview". See "Raising religion: It's delicate but sometimes necessary", Office of the Ombudsman, January 21, 2014.

Oldenbarneveld interview of Ayaan Hirsi Ali in Ottawa: https://youtu. be/FIIrHYWXKJQ

Oldenbarneveld launch of Tarek Fatah's book: http://gayandright. blogspot.ca/2010/10/politically-correct-lucy-van.html

Oldenbarneveld interview of Irshad Manji: https://soundcloud.com/ ottawa-writersfestival/irshad-manji-ottawa-sept-21

CBC on Charlie Hebdo: Christie Blatchford, "When push comes to shove, isn't it curious how it's always about the Jews?" National Post, January 9, 2015.

Death by China and the CBC: Greg Autry, "Canada: Democracy with Chinese Characteristics," November 20, 2012; http://www.gregautry.us/archives/1256.

"Clearly, a pro-Israeli lobby is active": Office of the Ombudsman, French Services "Mandate of the Office of the Ombudsman: Looking to the Future," August 9, 2007.

"a very well organized lobby": http://www.honestreporting.ca/radio-canada-ombudsman-annual-report-there-exists-real-problems-in-coverage-of-israeli-palestinian-conflict/13030

Pierre Tourangeau testimony: Standing Senate Committee for Transport and Communications, September 30, 2014.

Presentation of Steven Guiton to the Standing Senate Committee on Transport and Communications: http://www.parl.gc.ca/content/sen/committee/412/TRCM/Briefs/2015-02-02CBCMedia_Environment2014_e.pdf.

"Justin Trudeau 'thrills' Liberal crowd in Thunder Bay, Ont." CBC News, February 9, 2015.

"Canadians wants high-quality information": "New-look CBC aims for the hip," Toronto Star, January 6, 2006.

CBC Annual Public Meeting 2011: http://www.cbc.radio-canada.ca/en/reporting-to-canadians/annual-public-meeting/annual-public-meeting-2011/

Chapter 8. My Dinner with David

Hege Storhaug, *But the Greatest of These is Freedom: The Consequences of Immigration in Europe* (CreateSpace, 2011).

David Solway, *The Big Lie: On Terror, Antisemitism, and Identity* (Lester, Mason & Begg, 2007).

Clifford May, "Islamology 101" (National Review, December 6, 2012)

Bassam Tibi, *Islamism and Islam* (Yale University Press, 2012).

Jonathan Kay, *Among The Truthers* (Harper Perennial, 2011).

Counter-Jihad mini-convention in Brussels: http://counterjihadreport. com/2012/07/12/brussels-process-launched-by-the-international-civil-liberties-alliance-on-9-july-2012/

Gavin Boby's website: http://lawandfreedomfoundation.org/

Boby pitched his services: Larisa Brown, "'Mosque buster' claims he can stop 'tide of Islam' by giving free advice on how to block building plans for new places of worship," The Daily Mail Online, January 13, 2013.

Policing of EDL marches: Divya Talway, "Cost of policing EDL protests a 'considerable concern'," BBC News, July 19, 2013.

EDL violence: Ben Hurst, "EDL rioters who terrorised Birmingham city centre jailed for more than 75 years," Birmingham Mail, January 9, 2015.

Boby stopping Ahmadiyya mosque: Number 2 on his list – the Uxbridge Mosque – is Ahmadiyya. http://lawandfreedomfoundation.org/progress-so-far-9/.

Boby quote on "propagating Islamic doctrine": http://www.mrctv.org/videos/gavin-boby-brussels-icla-conference-july-9-2012.

Fred Litwin and Salim Mansur, "Mistaking Islamism for Islam," The Ottawa Citizen, January 29, 2013.

Janice Fiamengo, "Gavin Boby not misguided," The Ottawa Citizen, February 4, 2013.

CAIR-CAN tries to stop Boby: Robert Sibley, "CAIR-CAN's opposition to 'mosquebuster' speech still smacks of indirect intimidation," Ottawa Citizen blogs, February 4, 2013.

Boby quote on shoes in mosque: Kelly Roche, "Live News" 'Mosque-buster Gavin Boby in Ottawa," Ottawa Sun, February 4, 2013.

Boby's trip report on Canada: http://lawandfreedomfoundation.org/2013/02/17/blame-canada/.

Solway in PJ Media: David Solway, "Revisiting the Neighborhood,"

PJMedia, February 9, 2014.

Criticism of Bassam Tibi: David Solway, "Saving the Neighbourhood," FrontPage Magazine, February 15, 2013.

Ayaan Hirsi Ali on political Islam: Ayaan Hirsi Ali, "Swearing In the Enemy," The Wall Street Journal, May 18, 2013.

Pamela Geller in Toronto: Terry Davidson, "Pamela Geller speech still a go for Toronto," Toronto Sun, May 2, 2013.

Toronto Board of Rabbis on Geller: JTA, "Pamela Geller's Invitation to Speak in Toronto Angers Board of Rabbis," Forward.com, May 15, 2013.

Pamela Geller's website: Her blog Atlas Shrugs has moved to PamelaGeller.com

Elena Kagan in Nazi uniform: http://pamelageller.com/2010/07/shocking-kagans-princeton-thesis-cited-german-socialist-who-endorsed-nazis.html/

Geller saying Muslims have sex with goats: She says on her website that she put up this video in error and "was removed within moments of being put up." http://pamelageller.com/rebuttals-to-false-charges/

Malcolm X impregnating Ann Dunham: http://pamelageller.com/2008/10/how-could-stanl.html/

Obama had sex with a crack whore: http://pamelageller.com/2009/08/cnn-tells-sells-more-lies-about-palin-its-time-to-expose-the-truth-about-obama.html/

Geller on Srebinica: http://pamelageller.com/2011/06/srebrenica-unveiled.html/

Geller on birther theories: http://pamelageller.com/2008/10/how-could-stanl.html/

Daniel Pipes, "Islam vs. Islamism," Ottawa Citizen, May 3, 2014.

Pamela Geller, "Pamela Geller, WND Column: Daniel Pipes is Wrong on Islamic Jew-Hatred" http://pamelageller.com/2013/05/pamela-geller-wnd-column-daniel-pipes-is-wrong-on-islamic-jew-hatred.html/

Bostom challenge to Daniel Pipes: http://www.andrewbostom.org/blog/2013/05/20/i-have-agreed-to-debate-daniel-pipes-on-his-conception-of-islamic-antisemitism/.

David Solway, "Are We Tired of Fighting," PJMedia, June 4, 2013.

Krauthammer on Geert Wilders: Charles Krauthammer, "Krauthammer's Take," March 9, 2010.

Robert Spencer on Krauthammer: http://www.jihadwatch.org/2010/03/krauthammer-on-wilders-ignorant-naive-and-wrong

Robert Spencer's Master's Degree: Spencer earned a Master's Degree in Religious Studies from the University of North Carolina at Chapel Hill and wrote his thesis on Catholic Church history. http://webcat.lib.unc.edu/record=b2172870~S1

Tarek Fatah, *The Jew is Not My Enemy* (Signal, 2011).

Pamela Geller, "Where are the 'Moderate' Muslims?" Breitbart, May 28, 2013.

David Solway, "The Question of Islamic Reform," FrontPage Mag, July 12, 2013.

Paul Berman, *Terror and Liberalism* (W.W. Norton & Company, 2003).

Bernard Lewis on Islam and the Jews: Jonathan Sacks, "The Return of Anti-Semitism," The Wall Street Journal, January 30, 2015.

Robert Wistrich, *Antisemitism: The Longest Hatred* (Schocken Books, 1991).

Jeffrey Herf, *Nazi Propaganda for the Arab World* (Yale University Press, 2009).

Laura Payton, "Harper says 'overwhelmingly majority' agrees with Tories on niqabs," CBC News, March 12, 2015.

Laureen O'Neil, "Harper's niqab comments inspire snarky Twitter hashtag: #DressCodePM," CBC News, March 12, 2015.

"Israel's chief rabbi warns Dutch populist politician over kosher slaughter ban," Reuters, August 30, 2012.

Gates of Vienna on Jews and Geert Wilders: http://gatesofvienna. blogspot.ca/2012/08/whose-law.html

Story on banning of Islam in Angola: Jacob Mchangama, "The Opponents of Militant Islamism Are Often As Bigoted as Their Targets," The Daily Beast, December 7, 2013.

Jason Kenney in the House of Commons: Hansard, Thursday, March 26, 2015.

Nissan Ratzslav-Katz, "Indian Muslim Leaders Praise Israel During Official Visit," Arutz Sheva, August 21, 2007.

Bret Stephens, "The Last King of Java: Indonesia's former president offers a model of Muslim tolerance," The Wall Street Journal, April 9, 2007.

Paul Marshall and Nina Shea, *Silence: How Apostasy & Blasphemy Codes are Silencing Freedom Worldwide* (Oxford University Press, 2011).

Nasser Weddady and Sohrab Ahmari, *Arab Spring Dreams* (Palgrave Mcmillan Trade, 2012).

Gary G. Yerkey, "Siavosh Derakhti, a young Muslim, defends Jews and others targeted by hate crimes," Christian Science Monitor, November 15, 2013.

Ariel Ben Solomon, "Famous Egyptian writer says Hamas is 'the real enemy,' not Israel," The Jerusalem Post, December 18, 2014.

Roi Kais, "Egyptians want peace, says blogger visiting Israel," ynetnews.com, December 23, 2012.

Israel Today Staff, "Syrian Rebels Thank Netanyahu for Israel's Compassion," Israel Today, February 23, 2014.

Ariel Ben Solomon, "Syrian rebel groups congratulate Netanyahu on his election victory," The Jerusalem Post, March 20, 2015.

Qanta Ahmed, "Israel's jihad is mine," The Times of Israel blogs,

January 10, 2013.

Postscript

J.L. Granatstein, "How the Harper government lost its way on defence spending," Globe and Mail, October 1, 2014.

For more information on the state of the Canadian military, check The 3Ds Blog and the contributions of Mark Collins (cdfai3ds.wordpress.com).

hollow-point bullets: Zack Beauchamp, "Senator Rand Paul Touts False Claim from '9/11 Truth' Conspiracy Site," Thinkprogress.org, August 15, 2012.

Rand Paul on martial law: Michael Gerson, "Unmasking Rand Paul," Washington Post, February 5, 2015.

Bret Stephens, *America in Retreat: The New Isolationism and the Coming Global Disorder* (Sentinel, 2014).

Andrew Coyne, "Time for a new political party," Maclean's, March 6, 2011.

Conrad Black, *Rise To Greatness: The History of Canada from the Vikings to the Present* (McClelland & Stewart, 2014).

Made in the USA
Charleston, SC
27 August 2015